AF192102

Solomon Aggrey

The Golden Calf Generation

novum pro

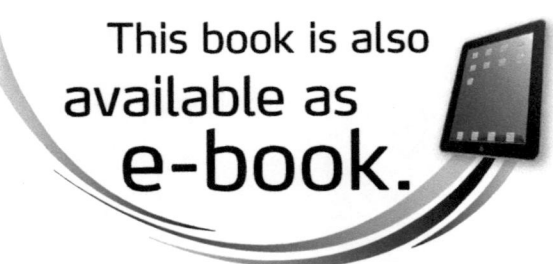

This book is also available as e-book.

www.novum-publishing.co.uk

© 2023 novum publishing

ISBN 978-3-99131-746-3
Editing: Atarah Yarach, DipEdit
Cover photo:
Leo Lintang | Dreamstime.com
Cover design, layout & typesetting:
novum publishing

www.novum-publishing.co.uk

Climate neutral
Print product
ClimatePartner.com/16547-2201-1002

Contents

Introduction

Then God said, 'Let us make man in Our image, according to Our likeness; let them have dominion over the fish of the seas, over the birds of the air, and over the cattle, over all the earth and over every creeping thing that creeps on the earth.' (Gen 1.26). So man, also the generic name for mankind, was made to be like God and to have His attributes in order to reveal His nature and His glory to all creation. The Psalmist says that man was made a little lower than God Himself and given dominion over all creation (Psa 8).

However, man disobeyed God and fell from his position. His constitution changed and he lost the special relationship he had with God. Man was no longer the image and the likeness of God but retained a poor impression of who he was before his fall. The devil, who himself had fallen away from God, was in charge of the world. But God, in His love for mankind, promised to restore man again. Speaking to the serpent, God said, 'And I will put enmity between you and the woman, and between your seed and her seed; He shall bruise your head, and you shall bruise His heel.'

After his fall, mankind became more corrupted. The gene pool of mankind became mixed up with others, especially with that of fallen angels, called the sons of God. The 'sons of God' birthed a hybrid race, the Nephilim, with earthly women, and they introduced more evil, wickedness, idolatry, violence and bloodshed. They corrupted the whole earth. So God destroyed the earth and every living thing on earth by flood, but Noah was found to be perfect and found grace in the sight of God (Gen 6.9, Gen 6.12). It means Noah was not corrupted by the Nephilim genes. As a result, God saved Noah and his household; Noah and his wife, his three sons and their wives. (1Pet 3.20, 2Pet 2.5). However, the Bible does not say anything about the righteousness of Noah's wife, his sons, and their wives.

The post-flood earth was repopulated by the descendants of the three sons of Noah; Shem, Ham and Japheth. Ham dishonoured his father, so Noah prophetically cursed Ham. 'Cursed be Canaan; a servant of servants he shall be to his brethren ... Blessed be the Lord God of Shem, and may Canaan be his servants. May God enlarge Japheth, and may he dwell in the tents of Shem; and may Canaan be his servants.' (Gen 9.25-27). As the descendants of Shem, Ham and Japheth were going to repopulate the earth, the curses and the blessings of Noah were also going to influence the whole course of human history, right to the end of time. Each of the sons had varying degrees of genetic contamination, but the greatest genetic contamination was found among the descendants of Ham.

It did not take very long, and the post-flood era became corrupt again. The Nephilim came back, especially among descendants of Ham, and the earth was once again filled with evil, wickedness, violence, idolatry, and bloodshed. Man drifted further and further away from God. God created man in His image and likeness to represent Him on the earth, in His power, in His glory and in His dominion. When Adam fell and changed his constitution, God updated the plan. Man would have to be transformed by faith into God's image and likeness through His Word. That was why the Word became flesh and dwelt among us. Jesus Christ was the last revelation of God on the earth. He came to the earth to give mankind the grace to be transformed once again in the image and the likeness of God through Him (Rom 8.29-30).

God chose a descendant of Shem called Abram and put into him the seed of Christ (the promise of salvation). Through Abram, all the families of the earth were to be blessed (Gen 12.3). God cut a covenant with Abram, that his descendants would be like the stars in heaven and the sand on the seashore. They would become strangers in a foreign land and serve them for four hundred years; after that He would free them and judge that nation (Gen 15.13-14). Abram gave birth to Isaac. Isaac gave birth to Jacob and Jacob gave birth to the fathers of the twelve tribes of Israel.

Yes, the children of Israel went to live in Egypt during a severe famine in the time of Joseph. After four hundred years, God set them free through the hand of Moses. Moses, by God's instruction, took the children of Israel to meet with Him on Mount Sinai before going to possess the Promised Land. After fifty days, through the Red Sea and the wilderness, the children of Israel stood before God on Mount Sinai. God made a covenant with the children of Israel to be their God and the children of Israel to be His people. He called Moses to the top of Mount Sinai and Moses was there forty days and forty nights to receive more revelation concerning the covenant.

Before Moses returned from the top of Mount Sinai to the camp, the children of Israel moulded a golden calf and worshipped it, right before the presence of the glory of God. The golden calf was a symbol of Baal, the male fertility god of the Canaanites. The children of Israel started out from Egypt as a nation without leaven (sin), now they were filled with leaven. They committed a great sin by breaking the covenant which God had cut with them. God was very angry with them but through the intercession of Moses, the children of Israel were allowed to continue their journey to the Promised Land. Baal worship never left the hearts of the children of Israel.

This book reveals the hidden code in the golden calf episode in the wilderness. The golden calf episode points to the generation before the return of Jesus Christ. That generation, the golden calf generation, will again worship and serve Baal. Many people today would not see themselves as Baal worshippers because our civilisation is different from the civilisation of the Canaanites. But our actions and behaviour indicate that we are worshipping and serving the same ancient gods of Baal, Ashtoreth and Molech.

Foreword

The episode of the golden calf in the Bible, chapter thirty-two, is one of the Biblical episodes many Christians know about. In this episode the children of Israel sinned against God by moulding and worshipping a golden calf while Moses was at the top of Mount Sinai with Jehovah God. God had spoken audibly to the children of Israel from the top of Mount Sinai about forty days prior to the incidence: 'I am the Lord your God who brought you out of the land of Egypt, out of the house of bondage. You shall have no other gods before Me. You shall not make for yourself a carved image – any likeness of anything that is in the heaven above, or that is in the earth beneath or that is in the water under the earth; you shall not bow down to them nor serve them. For, I, the Lord your God, am a jealous God…' (Exo 20.1-5). It was the beginning and the heart of the covenant which God ratified with the children of Israel.

The children of Israel trembled and drew back in fear at the sight of the glory of God and chose Moses as their mediator. The Bible says, 'The sight of the glory of the Lord was like a consuming fire on the top of the mountain in the eyes of the children of Israel.' Moses went up the mountain for forty days and forty nights, so he left deputies to take care of the needs of the children of Israel. On the thirty ninth day, just a day before Moses was supposed to come down from Mount Sinai, the children of Israel called to Aaron to make a god to go before them. Aaron moulded a golden calf, and they bowed down to it and served it. They disobeyed Jehovah God and broke the covenant they had cut with Him.

At the time the children of Israel made the golden calf, the glory of God could still be seen on the top of Mount Sinai, and it would have been very unusual and unnatural for the children of Israel to have ignored it altogether. But they did. It was as if Jehovah God was not present, or they had never known Him or never cut a covenant with Him. The fear of God which His divine and glorious presence was to instil in them was completely absent.

God was so provoked by the episode of the golden calf that He decided to destroy the children of Israel and raise another nation through Moses. But Moses pleaded with Him, and God in His great mercy changed His mind (Exo 32.11-14, Neh 9.18-21). On the fortieth day Moses descended from Mount Sinai with the first set of the tablets of the Ten Commandments written by God Himself. The Ten Commandments in the hands of Moses represented the image and likeness of God. The children of Israel were to live under the shadow of God's image and likeness so that they would be transformed and reflect Him on the earth. However, the children of Israel, just before Moses came down from Mount Sinai, chose the god they wanted to worship and serve. They chose the god whose image they would like to represent on the earth.

When Moses came down the mountain and saw what the children of Israel were doing, his own anger became so hot that he cast the tablets out of his hands and broke them at the foot of the mountain. The children of Israel really did not need the tablets, since they had already chosen another god to worship and serve. Moses took the golden calf, burnt it, ground it to powder, scattered it on water and made the children of Israel drink it.

The golden calf was the symbol of Baal, the Canaanite fertility god. When Joshua led the children of Israel across river Jordan into the Promised Land, he commanded the children of Israel, 'Now therefore, fear the Lord, serve Him in sincerity and in truth, and put away the gods which your fathers served on the other side of the river and in Egypt. Serve the Lord.' (Jos 24.14). In the Promised Land the children of Israel continued to worship and serve Baal. 'They forsook the Lord and served Baal and the Ashtoreths,' (Jud 2.13).

About 500 years after the golden calf episode at the foot of Mount Sinai, the first king of Samaria, Jeroboam, made two calves of gold and said to his people, 'It is too much for you to go up to Jerusalem. Here are your gods, O Israel, which brought you up from the land of Egypt.' (1Kin 12.28). He set up one calf in Bethel and the other in Dan. Jeroboam appointed feast days and priests and the people worshipped and served those calves. His intention was to prevent the people of his kingdom from going to Jerusalem to worship Jehovah God in the temple. The motive of Jeroboam exposed the purpose of the golden calf: to turn people away from following the true and living God.

In the Old Testament, God dealt with the types, the copies, the patterns, and the shadows of events which would take place in the New Testament. Apostle Paul says, 'So let no one judge you in food or in drink, or regarding a festival or a new moon or Sabbaths, which are a shadow of things to come but the substance is of Christ.' (Col 2.16-17). Jesus Christ was the final revelation of God, whose shadows and types appeared in the Old Testament.

Many of the things that happened to the children of Israel, especially in the wilderness, were foreshadowing of the things more fully revealed in the New Testament. 'Now all these things happened to them as examples, and they were written for our admonition, upon whom the ends of the ages have come.' (1Cor 10.11).

Moses was a type or the picture of the Redeemer, Jesus, the anointed. The children of Israel were a type of the Church. They were chosen as the priests of the world (Exo 19.5-6). Whatever happens to Israel eventually has a great effect on the whole world. Israel is like God's timing clock. The golden calf episode on Mount Sinai was a picture or a type of what would happen in the time of the end just before the return of Jesus Christ.

The people of Israel are expecting their Messiah for the first time and the Christians are expecting the return of their Messiah, our Lord Jesus Christ. The Israelites moulded the golden calf on the 39th day of Moses' ascension to the top of Mount Sinai, just a day before he came down. A day, prophetically, can be a period of time or a season. So, the period or the season before Jesus Christ returns, there will be an emergence of a golden calf generation.

In this period or season, many will fall away from worshipping the true and the living God and turn to Baal worship (including the worship of Molech and Ashtoreth). The worship of these ancient gods will drive the world's agenda and bring in a new unholy culture. Many world leaders will follow the sins of Aaron and Jeroboam, reject God's commandments, and cause people to follow other gods. They will institute ungodly laws to control the people who elected them and turn them away from the true God to worship man-made gods or national gods. Some of these leaders will persecute the church. Apostasy, idolatry and licentiousness will increase and multiply in the world.

What is happening around the world is not by accident. The rise of apostasy, idolatry, and the occult, the rise of the decriminalisation of abortion, the rise of homosexuality and legalisation of same-sex marriage can be linked to the ancient gods of Baal, Molech and Ashtoreth. It gives a prophetic indication that we are much closer to the return of our Jesus Christ than ever before. God said, 'Behold, I will send Elijah the prophet before the coming of the great and dreadful day of the Lord. And he will turn the hearts of the fathers to the children and the hearts of the children to their fathers.' (Mal 4.5-6). Prophet Elijah came headlong against the worship of Baal and Jezebel (Ashtoreth) in his day in order to turn many back to the true God. As Moses came down from Mount Sinai and destroyed the golden calf, so will the return of Jesus Christ bring judgement, destruction of idolatry, sin, and ungodliness and usher in a millennium age of rest and righteousness.

Chapter 1

The Seed Of Promise

The sin of Adam and Eve in the Bible altered the nature and the constitution of mankind and affected the whole earth. Apostle Paul says, 'Therefore, just as through one man sin entered the world, and death through sin, and thus death spread to all men, because all sinned... For all have sinned and fall short of the glory of God.' (Rom 5.12, Rom 3.23). Since the fall, violence, wickedness, corruption, and bloodshed have never left the earth. The aim for which God made man in His image and likeness was being defeated. God made man in His image, according to His likeness to represent Him and reveal His nature to all creation in such a way that His glory would be seen on earth (Gen 1.26, Psa 8.5-6).

The human race needed to be redeemed, but this redemption could not be achieved through its fallen Adamic nature. The only way was for man to be transformed by faith into the image of God's Son through the Word. 'And the Word became flesh and dwelt among us, and we beheld His glory, the glory as of the only begotten of the Father, full of grace and truth.' (Joh 1.14). 'Therefore, in all things He had to be made like His brethren, that He might be a merciful and faithful High Priest in things pertaining to God, to make propitiation for the sins of the people.' (Heb 2.17). The Saviour of the world, the Redeemer, the Christ, had to be like man in order to save the human race.

Jehovah God therefore needed someone on earth to carry the seed of Christ, the promised seed of salvation. The gene pool of the whole world was corrupted. The hearts of humanity were filled with violence, evil, wickedness, apostasy, and idolatry.

God sovereignly reached down in love and mercy and chose one of the descendants of Shem, called Abram, to carry the seed of Christ (1Chr 1.24-28, Gen 11.10-26, Gal 3.16). Abram had a fallen Adamic nature, like any human being, and was also an idol worshipper at that time (Jos 24.2-3). However, God chose him to begin a completely new godly generation, through whom the divine promise, the seed of the woman, who would bless all the families of the earth would come.

Now the Lord had said to Abram: 'Get out of your country, from your family and from your father's house to a land that I will show you. I will make you a great nation; I will bless you and make your name great and you shall be a blessing. I will bless those who bless you, and I will curse those who curse you; and in you all the families of the earth shall be blessed.' (Gen 12.1-3).

Stephen, one of the early disciples of Jesus, reminded the Sanhedrin before whom he stood indicted that God first called out Abram when he was in the Ur of the Chaldees. God told Abram to forsake his country, his relatives and his father's house to a land He would show him, and He would bless him, make his name great and a blessing. (Acts 7.2-4). Abram received the call of God and told his father, Terah. Terah had three sons: Abram, Nahor, and Haran. Haran died in the Ur of the Chaldees and left a son called Lot. Terah, as the head of the family, took Abram, their wives and Lot and moved first to dwell in Haran. Abram's wife, Sarai, who travelled with him, was barren and could not bring forth a son in the Ur of the Chaldees.

In Haran Abram received another call to leave, and he left with his wife, Sarai, and Lot, his nephew, when he was seventy-five years old. God led them over about 1500 miles to the land of Canaan, the Promised Land, which at that time was inhabited by the Canaanites. After a while both Abram and Lot became rich with flocks and herds, so there was constant strife between their herdsmen. Abram told Lot to choose any land he wanted and separate himself. Lot lifted his eyes and saw the plains of Jordan, and they were well watered and fruitful. So, he chose the plains of Jordan and journeyed east. But in the plains of Jordan were the cities of Sodom, Gomorrah, Admah, and Ziboiim, which God destroyed with brimstone and fire (Deu 29.23). When Lot separated himself from Abram, God reiterated to Abram the promise in more details.

'Lift your eyes now and look from the place where you are – northward, southward, eastward and westward; for all the land which you see I give to you and your descendants forever. And I will make your descendants as the dust of the earth; so that if a man could number the dust of the earth, then your descendants also could be numbered. Arise, walk in the land through its length and its width, for I give it to you.' (Gen 13.14-17).

Lot could not have been part of Abram's calling because Lot lived by sight, while Abraham lived by faith. In the process of time, the king of Sodom and four other Canaanite kings were joined together in a battle with Chedorlaomer, king of Elam (Persia) and his three allied kings. Chedorlaomer and his allied kings defeated the five Canaanite kings and took their goods and provisions and departed with Lot, who was living in Sodom.

When Abram was told of the capture of his nephew, he armed 318 trained servants who were born in his own house and went in pursuit of the four foreign kings (Gen 14.13-14). Abram went into the battle with courage and faith in his covenant God. He mounted a surprise attack and defeated the four kings and brought back his nephew, Lot, and all the other captives and their goods (Gen 14.16).

When Abram returned from his victory, he was met by two kings. The first was the defeated king of Sodom, called *Bera*. Bera means 'gift' or 'son of evil' according to Easton Dictionary. The second king who came to meet Abram was Melchizedek, the king of Salem.

'Then Melchizedek king of Salem brought out bread and wine; he was the priest of God Most High.' (Gen 14.18).

The Hebrew word 'Melchizedek' comes from *melek*, meaning king, and *tsedeq* meaning righteousness. The name Melchizedek might have been his title, the king of righteousness. In Heb 7.2, Melchizedek is also referred to as the king of Salem. Salem means peace. So Melchizedek was the king of righteousness, the king of peace, and the priest of God Most High.

Psalms 76.2 says, 'In Salem also is His tabernacle and His dwelling place in Zion.' Salem was the old name of Jerusalem. However, at that time, the earthly tabernacle of God had not been built yet and Zion (part of Jerusalem, referring to the governmental seat of God (Mic 4.2, Isa 2.3)) was also not established. So, I believe that Melchizedek was a heavenly king and priest. As a heavenly king, Melchizedek had divine authority in the areas of righteousness and peace and a seat in the government of God. His office might have been both heavenly and earthly in nature. As a priest he was the constant mediator and intercessor before God on behalf of Salem prior to the Aaronic priesthood.

God needed a perfect seed-line, but there was none on earth. In the pre-flood era, Noah was declared perfect; without genetic corruption before he and his household were saved from the flood judgment. In the post-flood era, no one was declared perfect. The whole earth was once again corrupt. Abram, whom God had chosen, was far from perfect. His DNA and bloodline were also corrupted through his lineage and through his idol worship (Jos 24.2-3). God took Abram from his family and country and led him to the Promised Land inhabited by the Canaanites who were also idol worshippers of the worse kind.

God had made promises to Abram that He would make him great and bless him, and that in him all the families of the earth would be blessed (Gen 12.1-3). If the DNA of Abram remained corrupted, then his seed would also be corrupted. The earth could not be blessed through him in that condition. Abram had to have a perfect, unpolluted, and uncorrupted DNA to bring forth a pure seed. But how? God already had an answer to that contingency. 'Then Melchizedek, king of Salem brought bread and wine; he was the priest of God Most High.' Apostle Paul describes Melchizedek as 'king of righteousness, king of peace, without father, without mother, without genealogy, having neither beginning of days nor end of life, but made like the Son of God, remains a priest continually.' (Heb 7.2-3).

'Without father, without mother and without genealogy,' indicates that Melchizedek had no Adamic sin or generational sins to deal with; no genetic corruption or pollution. In order words, Melchizedek had a perfect DNA. His DNA was like Adam before his fall or like the last Adam, Jesus Christ. Melchizedek, 'made like the Son of God,' tells us that he was a representation of God, a type of the Son of God, Jesus Christ.

Jesus Christ was born of Virgin Mary. He was not born of an earthly father. Jesus Christ, like Melchizedek, didn't have any Adamic sin, no generational sin, and no corrupted DNA. The angel Gabriel told Mary, 'The Holy Spirit will come upon you and the power of the highest will overshadow you; therefore, also that Holy One who is to be born will be called Son of God.' (Luk 1.35). Jesus Christ was not conceived by insemination but conceived by overshadowing.

The Father of Jesus was God and Jesus Christ's body and blood bore the record of God's DNA on earth. 'In the beginning was the Word, and the Word was with God, and the Word was God.' (Joh 1.1). 'And the Word became flesh and dwelt among us.' (Joh 1.14). Jesus Christ was and is also a King. The wise men from the East said, 'Where is He who has been born King of the Jews? For we have seen His star in the East and have come to worship Him.' (Mat 2.2, Zech 9.9). Jesus Christ Himself confirmed it before

Pilate by saying, 'My kingdom is not of this world.' (Joh 18.36-37). Jesus Christ was the antitype of Melchizedek. He is not our Pastor as people think, but our High Priest according to the order of Melchizedek (Psa 110.4, Heb 7.21, Heb 4.14-15). Jesus Christ was and is a King Priest, just like Melchizedek.

The true meaning of the bread and wine Melchizedek brought to Abram was not revealed until Jesus Christ came about 3,000 years later. He said, 'For the bread of God is He who comes down from heaven and gives life to the world … I am the bread which came down from heaven … This is the bread which comes down from heaven, that one may eat of it and not die … Most assuredly, I say to you, unless you eat the flesh of the Son of man and drink His blood, you have no life in You. Whoever eats My flesh and drinks My blood has eternal life, and I will raise him up at the last day. For My flesh is food indeed, and My blood is drink indeed. He who eats My flesh and drinks My blood abides in Me and I in him.' (Joh 6.33-56).

Many disciples of Jesus Christ did not understand and turned away from Him, but He explained it to them later. 'It is the Spirit who gives life; the flesh profits nothing. The words that I speak to you are spirit, and they are life.' (Joh 6.63). At Jesus Christ's last celebration of the Passover before He went to the cross, He took bread and broke it and said, 'Take, eat, this is my body.' He took the cup containing the wine and said, 'Drink from it, all of you. For this is My blood of the new covenant which is shed for the remission of sins.' (Mat 26.26-28). His disciples were not supposed to eat the physical body of Jesus Christ and drink His physical blood, but to eat the bread and drink the wine by faith.

Apostle Paul also delivered to the church his revelation: 'For I received from the Lord that which I also delivered to you; that the Lord Jesus on the same night in which He was betrayed took bread; and when He had given thanks, He broke it and said, 'Take, eat; this is My body which is broken for you; do this in remembrance of Me.' In the same manner He also took the cup after supper, saying, 'This cup is the new covenant in My blood. This do, as often as you drink it, in remembrance of Me. For as often as you eat this bread and drink this cup, you proclaim the Lord's death till He comes.' (1Cor 11.23-26). Jesus Christ instituted what we Christians usually call the Holy Communion.

To proclaim was to publicly announce, show forth, and exhibit Christ's suffering and death and to identify and profess oneness with it by faith through eating the bread and drinking the wine. The institution of the Holy Communion happened after the partaking of the Passover meal, as seen in the gospel according to Luke (Luk 22.14-20). Therefore, Jesus Christ set up a completely new covenant, different from the Passover. This new covenant, the Holy Communion, completely replaced the feast of Passover and was supposed to continue till Jesus Christ returns. Jesus Christ was the last Passover Lamb, so Passover was no longer meant to be celebrated by Christians after the death of Jesus Christ.

Jehovah God promised the Israelites a new covenant. "Behold, the days are coming,' says the Lord, 'when I will make a new covenant with the house of Israel and with the house of Judah – not according to the covenant that I made with their fathers in the day when I took them by the hand to lead them out of the land of Egypt…" (Heb 8.8-9). Jesus Christ became the Mediator of this new covenant by means of His death. 'And for this reason He is the Mediator of a new covenant, by means of death, for the redemption of the transgressions under the first covenant, that those who are called may receive the promise of the eternal inheritance. For where there is a testament, there must also of necessity be the death of the testator. For a testament is in force after men are dead, since it has no power at all while the testator lives.' (Heb 9.15-17).

So, it was only after the death of Jesus Christ that the new covenant came into force. Apostle Paul says that the new covenant was better because it was made on better promises. 'But now He obtained a more excellent ministry, inasmuch as he is also a mediator of a better covenant, which was established on better promises.' (Heb 8.6). Jesus Christ fulfilled the feast of Passover and set up a new covenant by His death. Because of that, the feast of Passover became obsolete to Christians (Heb 8.12-13).

Passover, to the Jews, was an annual celebration, and the Holy Communion to the Christians was and is celebrated as often as possible. When we proclaim the Lord's death by faith and become identified and one with it by eating the bread and drinking the wine, straight away we become also identified and one with the resurrection of Jesus Christ by faith. We have now entered into a completely different realm. Resurrection is life and He who gives life is the Holy Spirit. The Holy Spirit already dwells in every true believer. 'Now if anyone does not have the Spirit of Christ, he is not His.' In other words, he is not a Christian. 'Or do you not know that your body is the temple of the Holy Spirit who is in you, whom you have from God, and you are not your own?' (1Cor 6.19).

Remember Jesus Christ said, 'It is the Spirit who gives life.' When one takes the bread and the wine (Holy Communion) with the right intent, understanding and faith, the Holy Spirit begins to quicken the body. 'But if the Spirit of Him who raised Jesus from the dead dwells in you, He who raised Christ from the dead will also give life to your mortal bodies through His Spirit who dwells in you.' (Rom 8.11). 'He redeemed us from the curse of the law, that the blessing of Abraham might come upon the Gentiles in Christ Jesus, that we might receive the promise of the Spirit through faith.' (Gal 3.13-14, Gal 3.29).

The Holy Spirit begins to gradually execute the promises of the new covenant. And the greatest benefit of the new covenant is to be transformed into the same image and likeness of Christ. 'But we all, with unveiled face, beholding as in a mirror the glory of the Lord, are being transformed into the same image from glory to glory, just as by the Spirit of the Lord.' (2Cor 3.18). You see, the Holy Communion, if properly taken, is able to initiate our transformation to become like Christ, without father, without mother, without genealogy. That is, it is able to change our corrupt and tainted DNA to that of Christ's incorruptible body, making Holy Communion completely different from Passover.

Apostle Paul explains, 'For we know that the whole creation groans and labours with birth pangs together until now. Not only that, but we also who have the first fruits of the Spirit, even we ourselves groan within ourselves, eagerly waiting for the adoption, the redemption of our body. For we are saved in this hope, but hope that is seen is not hope; for why does one still hope for what he sees?' (Rom 8.22-24). Every true believer can tell you that by grace we have been saved through faith (Eph 2.8). But Apostle Paul takes us a step further. He intimates that the purpose of our salvation by faith is the adoption and the redemption of our bodies through hope. Salvation by faith is instantaneous but the redemption of the body is through hope. It is a process and takes time.

Jesus Christ told His Jewish audience, 'Your father Abraham rejoiced to see My day, and he saw it and was glad.' (Joh 8.56). The Jews questioned Him because Abraham had long died and gone. Jesus replied, 'Most assuredly, I say to you before Abraham was, I AM.' (Joh 8.58). From this I see that Abraham was able to connect the bread and the wine Melchizedek brought him to the final redemption through the suffering, death, and resurrection of Jesus Christ. He saw the transformation from the corrupted human nature to the incorruptible resurrected nature of Jesus Christ. Abraham rejoiced to see the end-fruit of the bread and the wine.

The church has emphasised salvation to such an extent that it has completely overshadowed or obliterated the true purpose of our salvation. The first time the truth dawned on me, I was shocked. It looked as if it was a new truth, but it wasn't. It looks as if many Christians have been programmed to ignore this revelation, the true purpose of their salvation. So the revelation of it is missing in our churches.

The new covenant includes changing our natural body to conform to the body of Christ, not while we are dead but while we are still alive. And the partaking of the Holy Communion with proper intent, understanding and faith plays a major role in it. It is sad that our fathers and many Christians treat the Holy Communion as an extension of the feast of Passover. I did for a long time, until the revelation hit me. If we hook the Holy Communion to the feast of Passover, we receive nothing from it. No life comes of it. It becomes useless because the Holy Communion is completely under a new covenant.

God, through Melchizedek, laid a solid foundation for the seed of Abraham to be transformed and become perfect like His Son, Jesus Christ. 'For whom He foreknew, He also predestined to be conformed to the image of His Son, that He might be the first-born among many brethren. Moreover whom He predestined, these He also called; whom He called these He also justified and whom He justified these He also glorified.' (Rom 8.29-30). This is the main purpose why we are in this world. Not just to be born again, but to appropriate the grace to be transformed into the image and likeness of Christ; to return to who we were initially.

When people of the New Testament condemn and cast aside the Old Testament, what they don't realise is that they are shooting themselves in the foot. The whole plan of God's salvation of mankind through Jesus Christ began with one man, Abraham. 'Now to Abraham and his Seed were the promises made. He does not say, 'And to your seeds', as of many, but as of one, 'And to your Seed,' who is Christ … And if you are Christ's, then you are Abraham's seed, and heir according to the promise.' (Gal 3.16, Gal 3.29).

Melchizedek then blessed Abram: 'Blessed be Abram of God Most High, possessor of heaven and earth; and blessed be God Most High who had delivered your enemies into your hand. And he gave him a tithe.' (Gen 14.19-20).

Melchizedek, in accordance with his priestly office, blessed Abram. The blessing carried with it the power of succession and endowment to the next generation. Abraham blessed his son, Isaac, Isaac blessed Jacob, and Jacob blessed Judah, and so on. So, the divine succession and endowment continued until Christ, the true Seed of Abraham was born. Jehovah's covenant promises to Abraham included the blessing of all the families of the earth. 'And in you all the families of the earth shall be blessed.'

The God Most High is El Elyon in Hebrew. El Elyon means the highest, the first, the uppermost and pre-eminent in every position and rank. No one and nothing is higher than El Elyon. There are three distinct attributes of the God Most High revealed by the blessing of Melchizedek.

1. El Elyon is the possessor of heaven and earth. Everything in heaven and earth belongs to El Elyon, the land, the mineral, mankind, animals etc. All that man owns belongs to El Elyon (Deu 10.14, Psa 89.11). This is kingdom language. In other words, El Elyon is like a king, having a sovereign and supreme authority over everything in His domain. It is very important to grasp and understand this. 'We brought nothing into this world, and it is certain we can carry nothing out.' (1Tim 6.7). Paul asks, 'What do you have that you did not receive?' (1Cor 4.7). King Nebuchadnezzar learnt the hard way that the God Most High was the possessor of heaven and earth. As a result of his pride, God drove him out of his palace into the forest. He lived like an animal for seven years. At the end of the seven years his understanding returned, and he recognised that El Elyon was the Possessor of heaven and earth. 'I, Nebuchadnezzar, lifted my eyes to heaven, and my

understanding returned to me; and I blessed the Most High and praised and honoured Him who lives forever: For His dominion is an everlasting dominion, and His kingdom is from generation to generation.' (Dan 4.35, see also Dan 5.23-31).

2. As the possessor of heaven and earth, El Elyon has the right to give, withhold or distribute his possession in heaven and on earth to whom He chooses. It was El Elyon who divided the Promised Land between the children of Israel according to their numbers. (Deut 32.8).

3. El Elyon is also a powerful redemptive name. He redeemed Abram from the four powerful kings of the East. It was El Elyon who delivered Shadrach, Meshach, and Abednego from the burning fiery furnace (Dan 3.26, 29). The Psalmist says, 'Then they remembered that God was their rock and the Most High God their Redeemer.' (Psa 78.35). In a song of David, it was El Elyon who uttered His voice and moved in battle to redeem him. (2Sam 22.14)

The God who revealed Himself to Abraham was El Shaddai. 'I appeared to Abraham, to Isaac and to Jacob as God Almighty...' (El Shaddai) (Exo 6.3). El Shaddai is an All-sufficient God, who is more than enough. He gives, He blesses, He satisfies and nourishes. Nothing is lacking in *El Shaddai* and nothing is impossible to Him. Through Melchizedek, God manifested Himself to Abram as El Elyon, the Possessor of heaven and earth.

The Psalmist says, 'He who dwells in the secret place of the Most High, shall abide under the shadow of the Almighty.' (Psa 91.1). The word Almighty is a Hebrew translation of Shaddai. The secret place of El Elyon is His covering, His hiding place or where one will find Him. God is pure light without any darkness and therefore produces no shadow. The shadow of God may be likened to the benefits one receives when under a tree; that is under His hand. In other words, when one comes under His covering, His protection, His nourishing, and His nurturing of El Shaddai. Now let's try to understand the verse.

Anybody who comes into the hiding place, or the covering of El Elyon shall also come under the protection, the covering, nourishing and the nurturing of El Shaddai. It shows that El Elyon works through El Shaddai for the full provision of God's blessing. With this combined revelation of God as El Shaddai and El Elyon, the seed of Abraham was to be as the stars of the heaven and the sand on the seashore and Abraham would have the ability to possess the gates of his enemies. And in his seed, all the nations of the earth shall be blessed (Gen 22.17-18). Melchizedek was sent by the God Most High, El Elyon, to Abram with bread and wine, symbolising the body and the blood of Jesus Christ so that Abram could be seeded by Christ. The Seed of Christ was sown in Abram so that he could be perfect and physically birth a perfect seed, Jesus Christ, through whom the whole earth will be blessed. Marvellous! What a plan!

There are many Christians and even ministers of God who believe that Jesus Christ paid everything on the cross so that they don't have to do anything. It sounds religious and gives the impression that they are putting all their faith in Christ, but it is a big deception. Apostle Peter, one of the twelve disciples of Jesus Christ, who walked with Him, saw his crucifixion and his resurrection, says, 'For to this you were called, because Christ also suffered for us, leaving us an example that you should follow His steps.' (1Pet 2.21). Every true Christian is required to sacrifice for the sake of Jesus Christ. All the apostles of Jesus Christ except Apostle John were martyred in different nations.

Jesus Christ said Himself, 'If anyone desires to come after Me; let him deny himself, and take up his cross daily and follow Me. For whoever desires to save his life will lose it, but whoever loses his life for My sake will save it.' (Luk 9.23-24). You've got to deny or lose your very self in order to gain Christ. No one can do it for you. Apostle Paul says, 'Yet indeed I also count all things loss for the excellence of the knowledge of Christ Jesus my lord, for whom I have suffered the loss of all things, and count them as rubbish, that I may gain Christ.' (Phil 3.8).). I can go on and on, but my point is to emphasise a powerful spiritual law. Nothing is free. You have to sacrifice something to gain something better or greater.

You can call it a sowing, a trading, or even a leverage. What you put in, lose, or sow is smaller compared with what you receive or gain. Jesus said, 'Take my yoke upon you and learn from Me, for I am gentle and lowly in heart, and you will find rest for your souls. For My yoke is easy and My burden is light.' (Mat 11.29–30). The yoke under normal conditions is heavy, a big constraint or a bondage to one's life, yet the yoke of Christ is easy, light and gives one rest. Yes, you've got to take the yoke of Christ and put it upon yourself. Yes, there will be some discomfort and some sacrifice, but what you gain is far greater. 'For I consider that the suffering of this present time are not worthy to be compared with the glory which shall be revealed in us.' (Rom 8.18). So, in the long run, each person works out his/her own salvation by the choices he/she makes. (Phil 2.12). It is all about God, but each of us has to determine how far he/she wants to go with God.

When Abram received the bread, the wine, and the blessing of Melchizedek, he gave Melchizedek tithe of all the spoil. (Gen 14.20). It is the first time the word tithe has been used in the Bible. Tithe in Hebrew means a tenth or 10 percent. So, Abram gave to Melchizedek a tenth of all the spoil he took in his battle with the four foreign kings. The blessing of Melchizedek indicated that El Elyon delivered the four kings into the hands of Abram. It was not Abram's sole effort that won the battle; El Elyon plotted the defeat of the four kings and the victory of Abram.

According to Hastings Dictionary of the Bible and Fausset Bible Dictionary, the practice of offering tithes of the fruits of the field and of the flocks dates back to a period anterior to Israelite history. A tenth of the flocks, fruits, and possessions of all kinds, as well as the spoils of war, was considered sacred and given to the gods. It is not wrong to assume that Abram knew about the sacredness of tithing before he met Melchizedek.

El Elyon, as the Possessor of heaven and earth, owns everything, the land, the minerals, the animals and the people on earth, as we have mentioned. 'For every beast of the forest is Mine, and the cattle on a thousand hills. I know all the birds of the mountains, and the wild beasts of the field are Mine. If I were hungry, I would not tell you; for the world is Mine and all its fullness.' (Psa 50.10-12). El Elyon does not need any man to give Him anything; and Melchizedek did not ask for tithe, neither was there any law or compulsion for Abram to give or pay tithe. So why did Abram give tithe to Melchizedek? It was for Abram's own benefit. Abram gave a voluntary tithe to Melchizedek in response to receiving the bread, the wine, and the blessing.

1. Abram gave voluntary tithe to Melchizedek to thank God and honour El Elyon for all the help he had received from Him.
2. Abram gave voluntary tithe to Melchizedek because he recognised that the source of his victory and possessions was El Elyon.
3. Abram gave voluntary tithe to Melchizedek to affirm and seal what had taken place between him and Melchizedek. It was like a transaction. The Law which came about four hundred and thirty (430) years later could not annul that transaction (Gal 3.17).
4. By giving voluntary tithe to Melchizedek, Abram was connecting, sowing, trading into the kingdom of Melchizedek; the kingdom of peace and the kingdom of righteousness. Abram was saying, 'I and my seed are part or citizens of your kingdom.'
5. By giving voluntary tithe to Melchizedek, Abram invested and committed his seed to God's plan of redemption through Jesus Christ. 'And if you are Christ's, then you are Abraham's seed, and heirs according to the promise.'
6. By giving voluntary tithe to Melchizedek, Abram was confirming or activating a covenant of God's help in difficult times.

When Abram gave tithe to Melchizedek, he was carrying in his loins two nations or two seeds, the nation of Israel and the nation of the church through Jesus Christ. (1Pet 2.9). So, the seeds also gave tithe to Melchizedek and therefore shared and partook of the bread and wine (the body and the blood). 'Even Levi, who receives tithes, paid tithes through Abraham, so to speak, for he was still in the loins of his father when Melchizedek met him.' (Heb 7.10).

Abram gave voluntary tithe, but the Levites who were in his loins paid tithes under the Mosaic Law. Why? Because the constituent structure of peace and righteousness of Israel had already been laid or decided by Abram's tithe. In the case of the church, Jesus Christ fulfilled the Mosaic Law and set up a new covenant. The church was birthed through the death and the resurrection of Jesus Christ. Therefore, the church's commitment to Jesus Church went further than just paying tithe. It was a total sacrifice of oneself as a living sacrifice.

Abram and Sarai, being very advanced in age, could not naturally give birth to a son. Abram's wife, Sarai, gave her Egyptian maid, Hagar, to Abram and Abram had a son with her and called him Ishmael. But when Abram was ninety-nine years old, and Sarai ninety years, God appeared to Abram and said,

I am Almighty God; walk before me and be blameless. And I will make my covenant between Me and you, and will multiply you exceedingly … As for Me, behold, My covenant is with you, and you shall be a father of many nation. No longer shall your name be called Abram, but your name shall be Abraham; for I have made you a father of many nations … As for Sarai your wife, you shall not call her name Sarai, but Sarah shall be her name. And I will bless her and also give you a son by her; then I will bless her, and she shall be a mother of nations; kings of people shall be from her.
Gen 17. 1-16.

God told Abram, 'I am El Shaddai, walk before Me and be blameless.' It was a condition for being transformed into the image and likeness of Christ, apart from eating the bread and drinking the wine. The Hebrew word 'before' is *paniym*. *Paniym* means face, countenance, or presence. So, the passage can read, 'Walk or live in my face or in my presence continually and be blameless.' The word blameless in Hebrew is *tamiym,* translated as perfect, without blemish, upright, whole, entire, or sound. When one is perfect, it means one does not have genetic corruption; without father, without mother, without genealogy, having neither beginning of days nor end of life and made like the Son of God (Heb 7.3).

Now the face of El Shaddai was not on the earth but in heaven. To live in God's face or presence would mean Abram had to enter heaven and continually live before Him. How could Abram have lived in heaven and on earth at the same time? Is it possible? Yes. Jesus Christ lived here on earth while He was also at the same time in heaven (Joh 3.13). Apostle Paul says that man has a spiritual body which is separate from his natural body. 'It is sown a natural body, it is raised a spiritual body. There is a natural body, and there is a spiritual body.' (1Cor 15.44). The spiritual body lives in heaven and the natural body on earth. In other words, the natural body becomes an extension of the spiritual body.

It is the continuous living in the face of God that brings complete transformation of the body. Moses went up and stayed in God's presence for forty days and forty nights. When he came down from Mount Sinai, the skin of his face shone with the glory of God and the children of Israel were afraid to go near to him (Exo 34.29-32). 'But we all, with unveiled face, beholding as in a mirror the glory of the Lord, are being transformed into the same image from glory to glory, just as by the Spirit of the Lord.' (2Cor 3.18). Yes, it is possible. This is another revelation which has been hidden from many believers. God has been merciful to me, but my experience will definitely be different from yours; so it will be better for you to meditate on 1Cor 15.35-49 until the Holy Spirit shows you a way forward.

Abram did not complain about God's command to live continually in his face, but he laughed when God said He would give him a son by Sarai. He knew it was impossible, so he assumed that God was referring to Ishmael. But God said, "No, Sarah you wife shall bear you a son, and you shall call his name Isaac; I will establish My covenant with him for an everlasting covenant, and with his descendants after him.' (Gen 17.19).

God waited until Abram and Sarai had both passed the age of childbearing. Abram could not produce a sperm cell, nor Sarai produce an ovum or retain a child. Their reproductive organs were shut down, dead. But through faith Abraham (not Abram) and Sarah (not Sarai) were able to bring forth the promised son. Apostle Paul confirms, 'By faith Sarah herself also received strength to conceive seed, and she bore a child when she was past the age, because she judged Him faithful who had promised. Therefore, from one man, and him as good as dead, were born as many as the stars of the sky in multitude – innumerable as the sand which is by the seashore.' (Heb 11.11-12).

Isaac was born through the deadness of Abram and Sarai. He was the son of resurrection. God established the covenant of Abraham with Isaac and not with Ishmael, who was the firstborn. Isaac was born through faith (laughter) while Ishmael was born through the flesh. Ishmael was born of Abram, but Isaac was born of Abraham. Ishmael means God will hear and Isaac means laughter. And the seed of the promise of salvation passed from Abraham to Isaac. We can see Isaac as a type of the church, birthed from the death and resurrection of Jesus Christ. And we can also see him as a type of Christ, the seed of Abraham (Gal 3.16).

God decided to put Abraham to a test. 'Take now your son, your only son Isaac whom you love, and go to the land of Moriah, and offer him there as a burnt offering on one of the mountains of which I shall tell you.' (Gen 22.1-2). God had told Abraham that His covenant would be with Isaac and not with Ishmael. And now the same God was telling him to kill Isaac. God had already cut a covenant with Abraham, so Abraham put his full faith in His covenant God that even if Isaac died, God would raise him up again. His faith in the covenant was complete and unshakeable, so he offered up Isaac.

By faith Abraham, when he was tested, offered up Isaac, and he who had received the promises offered up his only begotten son, of whom it was said, 'In Isaac your seed shall be called,' concluding that God was able to raise him up, even from the dead, from which he also received him in a figurative sense (Heb 11.17-19).

The faith of Abraham was tried, proven, and perfected in the offering of his son, Isaac. It was not only to test whether Abraham would uphold the covenant. It was also to test that Abraham's soul-life was completely dead; that the love of his son was incapable of triggering any disobedience to God. This is a second condition for complete transformation into the image and likeness of Christ. The soul-life must die completely. 'He who loves father or mother more than Me is not worthy of Me. And he who loves son or daughter more than Me is not worthy of Me. And he who does not take his cross and follow after Me is not worthy of Me. He who finds his life will lose it, and he who loses his soul for My sake will find it.' (Mat 10.37-39, Luk 9.23-25).

On the way to the mount of Moriah, Abraham said to his servants, 'Stay here with the donkey; the lad and I will go yonder and worship, and we will come back to you.' (Gen 22.5). So the sacrifice of his son or the total denial of his soul-life was an act of worship to God. Isaac asked his father, Abraham, 'Look, the fire and the wood but where is the lamb for the burnt offering?' And Abraham said, 'My son, God will provide for Himself the lamb for a burnt offering.' (Gen 22.7-8).

At Mount Moriah, Abraham built an altar, tied Isaac and put him on it, and was about to sacrifice him when the angel of the Lord stopped him. 'Do not lay your hand on the lad or do anything to him; for now I know that you fear God...' When Abraham lifted his eyes, he saw a ram caught in a thicket by the horns. So Abraham took the ram and offered it ass a burnt offering instead of his son. God provided for Himself a lamb for a burnt offering, just as He gave Jesus Christ as His Passover Lamb.

Then the angel of the Lord called to Abraham a second time out of heaven and said,

By Myself I have sworn, says the Lord, because you have done this thing, and have not withheld your son, your only son – blessing I will bless you, and multiplying I will multiply your descendants as the stars of the heaven and as the sand which is on the seashore; and your descendants shall possess the gate of their enemies. In your seed all the nations of the earth shall be blessed, because you have obeyed My voice.
Gen 22.16-18

The sacrifice of Isaac was a seed for the nation of Israel and a picture of the sacrifice of Jesus Christ. 'For God so loved the world that He gave His only begotten Son, that whoever believes in Him should not perish but have everlasting life.' That supreme sacrifice brought a very great reward. 'Most assuredly, I say to you, unless a grain of wheat falls into the ground and dies, it remains alone; but if it dies, it produces much grain.' (Joh 12.24). Through the sacrifice of Isaac, God multiplied the descendants of Abraham as the stars of the heavens and as the sand on the seashore. Through the sacrifice of Jesus Christ, God received countless number of sons like Jesus Christ.

God does not swear because His word is enough, but here God swore. There was nothing higher He could swear to so God swore by Himself, that He would unconditionally fulfil the promise.

We also see here an additional detail that the descendants of Abraham will possess the gates of their enemies. Paul explains why God swore by Himself.

For when God made a promise to Abraham, because he could swear by no one greater, He swore by Himself, saying, 'Surely, blessing I will bless you, and multiplying I will multiply you. And so, after he had patiently endured, he obtained the promise. For men indeed swear by the greater, and an oath for confirmation is for them an end of all dispute. Thus God determining to show more abundantly to the heirs of promise the immutability of His counsel, confirmed it by an oath, that by two immutable things, in which it is impossible for God to lie, we might have strong consolation, who have fled for refuge to lay hold of the hope set before us. This hope we have as an anchor of the soul, both sure and steadfast, and which enters the Presence behind the veil, where the forerunner has entered for us, even Jesus, having become High Priest forever according to the order of Melchizedek. Heb 6.13-20

The promise of Abraham reached far beyond the physical land and the birth of a nation innumerable as the stars in the heavens and the sand on a seashore. The promise reached to the throne of God; a return, a reconciliation with God through his seed, Jesus Christ. Through the obedience of one man, Abraham, the promise of God's blessing was extended to all mankind through Jesus Christ.

The Christ-seed passed from Abraham to Isaac. Isaac had twins with Rebecca, his cousin. The first of the twins was Esau and the second was Jacob. However, the Christ-seed passed from Isaac to Jacob. Jacob fled from his brother Esau to Mesopotamia and married two sisters, Leah and Rachel. He had twelve sons with them and their maidservants. God changed the name of Jacob to Israel as he returned to the land of promise. The twelve sons of Israel, the children of Israel, became the fathers of the twelve tribes of Israel.

The children of Israel were in the loins of their father Abram when he met Melchizedek and partook of the bread and the wine. So, the children of Israel were covenanted to be perfect and to be transformed into the image and likeness of Christ. The promised seed continued to pass through the tribe of Judah, then Perez, through David and so on until the Seed came to Mary, the mother of Jesus and became flesh as Jesus, the Christ, through whom the whole earth will be blessed. Therefore, to the Jews, the children of Israel, belonged the gospel of Christ.

Jesus Christ rightly said, 'I was not sent except to the lost sheep of the house of Israel.' (Mat 15.24). He instructed His disciples, 'Do not go into the way of the Gentiles, and do not enter a city of the Samaritans. But go rather to the lost sheep of the house of Israel.' (Mat 10.5-6). When the children of Israel, to whom complete salvation was initially apportioned, rejected Jesus Christ, salvation came to the Gentiles (Rom 11.11-12). The Apostle explained that it was as if some of the branches of an olive tree were broken off and a wild olive tree were grafted in among them so that they could become a partaker of the root and the fatness of the olive tree (Rom 11.17). It was meant to be so, that through Abraham, the whole world might be blessed. God cautioned Peter about the gentiles, 'What God has cleansed you must not call common.'

A new spiritual nation therefore came into being after the death and the resurrection of Jesus Christ called ekklesia, the church. It partook of the same Godhead and the blessings of Abraham. But this new nation had a completely new covenant, capable of fulfilling God's plan of redemption through Jesus Christ. 'But you are a chosen generation, a royal priesthood, a holy nation, His own special people that you may proclaim the praises of Him who called you out of darkness into His marvellous light.' (1Pet 2.9).

The whole plan of salvation of mankind started with Abraham, but the heirs of the promise were not and are not only the descendants of Abraham but all those who walk in the faith of the promise of Abraham (Rom 4.10-12). Abraham lived spiritually far beyond his time into the age of the New Testament. 'And if you are Christ's, then you are Abraham's seed, and heir according to the promise.' (Gal 3.29).

Now, to Abraham and his seed were the promises made. He does not say, 'And to seeds,' as of many, but as of one, 'And to your Seed,' which is Christ. And this I say, that the law, which was four hundred and thirty years later, cannot annul the covenant that was confirmed before by God in Christ, that it should make the promise of no effect. For if the inheritance is of the Law, it is no longer of promise; but God gave it to Abraham by promise (Gal 3.16-17).

The complete salvation of the Gentiles was initially a mystery, hidden from the children of Israel but was revealed to Apostle Paul, 'that the Gentiles should be fellow heirs, of the same body, and partakers of His promise in Christ through the gospel.' (Eph 3.6).

Chapter 2

Israel in Egypt

Noah gave birth to three sons, Shem, Ham, and Japheth before the flood judgment (Gen 6.10). After the flood judgement, Ham dishonoured his father by not covering his father's nakedness, so Noah cursed him. 'Cursed be Canaan; the servant of servants he shall be to his brethren. Blessed be the Lord, the God of Shem, and may Canaan be his servant. May God enlarge Japheth. And may he dwell in the tent of Shem; and may Canaan be his servant.' (Gen 9.24-29).

Noah prophetically pronounced his last patriarchal blessings and curses on his three sons. Those blessings and curses would determine the courses and events of their lives and influence the whole course of human history, right to the end of time. Canaan was the fourth son of Ham (Gen 10.6). But he was cursed instead of his father, who committed the sin. Noah cursed Canaan prophetically because the corruption of Canaan was going to overtake that of his father, Ham. In other words, the sins of Ham would find their fullness in the lives of the Canaanites. Historic facts would show that all the descendants of the sons of Ham were corrupted to some extent, but the greatest corruption was found among the descendants of Canaan.

The sons of Ham were Cush, Mizraim, Put, and Canaan (Gen 10.6). Mizraim was the original name given to Egypt by the Hebrews in the Old Testament. Scripture refers to Egypt as the land of Ham (Psa 105.27, Psa 106.22). So, Ham might have migrated to the land of Egypt initially with his son Mizraim. According to the Easton Dictionary, *Mizraim* means 'dual of Matzor' and *Matzor* means a mound, a fortress or people descended from Ham. The 'dual of Matzor' pointed to the two halves of Egypt, Upper Egypt and Lower Egypt. Upper Egypt was in the south and the Lower Egypt was in the north. Lower Egypt was sometimes referred to as the Matzor, and Upper Egypt, Papros. Together they formed the Mizraim (Is 19.6, Is 37.35, Is 11.11, Jer 44.1, Ezek 30.14). The river Nile ran through both the Upper and the Lower Egypt. The Nile originated from the highlands of Africa and passed through several countries like Uganda, Sudan, and Ethiopia before reaching Upper Egypt in the south and through to Lower Egypt in the north, where it divided into several branches to form the Nile delta and emptied into the Mediterranean Sea. The Nile is the longest river in the world and runs about 4200 miles from its sources to the Mediterranean.

The river Nile was and is a major source of water for many people. Wherever the river overflowed its banks, it produced a rich fertile land, so settlements were not very far away from the Nile. Upper Egypt was more of a desert, while Lower Egypt, because of the Delta, was very fertile and so heavily populated. Lower Egypt therefore saw more migrants and traders and was more familiar to the Canaanites and the Greeks. The migrants and the traders brought with them new knowledge, new culture, new art, and technology. So, the difference between Upper and Lower Egypt was not only geographical but also cultural, social, political and economic.

In ancient Egypt the two halves were ruled by different kings; they were virtually two independent kingdoms. The emblem of Upper Egypt was the vulture and the emblem of Lower Egypt was the cobra. According to historians, King Menes of Upper Egypt invaded Lower Egypt and unified the two Egypts politically around 3000 BC. He became the first monarch of the united Egypt. He chose the name Pharaoh and began wearing a double crown of the vulture and the cobra.

The capital of the ancient Egypt, before their unification, was Memphis, known as Noph in the Bible (Isa 19.13, Jer 2.16, Eze

30.13). In the 18th century BC, a group of non-Egyptians from Canaanite and Asiatic backgrounds, known as the Hyksos, migrated to the eastern part of Lower Egypt. From about 1630 BC they began to rule Egypt and set up their capital in the eastern part of Lower Egypt and called it Avaris, identified as Zoan in the Bible according to Smith Dictionary (Psa 78.43, Eze 30.14). They imposed their own Pharaohs (called Shepherd Kings), so the indigenous Pharaohs moved to Thebes in the south. In about 1520 BC, the Hyksos were routed and uprooted by the indigenous kings from Thebes, and so ended about 110 years of Hyksos reign.

Biblical chronology shows that Jacob entered Egypt about 1711 BC and the exodus of the children of Israel took place about 1496 BC. Therefore, the children of Israel migrated to Egypt at the time of the reign of the Hyksos. Among the 12 sons of Jacob, it was Joseph who first went to Egypt, and through him the whole family migrated there.

'Now Israel loved Joseph more than all his children, because he was the son of his old age. Also he made him a tunic of many colours. But when his brothers saw that their father loved him more than all his brothers, they hated him and could not speak peaceably to him.' (Gen 37.3-4). Joseph had dreams which indicated that members of his family would bow down to him in future; so, his brothers hated him even more.

Out of the deep envy and jealousy the brothers had developed for Joseph, they stripped him of his tunic and put him in a pit. They later sold him to the Ishmaelites on route to Egypt for twenty shekels of silver. They dipped his tunic in the blood of a goat and brought it to show their father, Jacob, that a wild animal had killed him. Jacob loved Joseph more than all his sons, so he mourned him for many days, knowing that he was dead.

In Egypt Joseph was sold to Potiphar, an officer of Pharaoh and captain of his guard. The Lord began to bless the house of Potiphar because of Joseph. In the house of Potiphar, Joseph had the privilege of learning Egyptian ethics and culture. He also became so proficient in economics and business administration that his wealthy master left everything he had in his hands.

However, the wife of Potiphar began to cast a longing eye on Joseph and asked him to 'lie with her,' but Joseph refused. A day came when the wife of Potiphar caught Joseph by his garment when no one was in the house, to lie with her. Joseph ran away and left his garment. So, the wife of Potiphar gathered his garment and shouted rape. Potiphar was very angry with Joseph when he heard it and put him in a special prison where the king's prisoners were kept.

Joseph was the most loved of his wealthy father in Canaan but was sold into slavery. In Egypt he had no identity and no will of his own, just an ordinary slave. His life was worth nothing, but he chose the fear of God above his own pleasure and interest and found himself in prison. Many of us would have been displeased that God had forsaken us. 'Well, I did a good thing for not sleeping with my master's wife and look at what it has landed me.' 'God gave me a dream that I was going to rule over my brothers. Look at me now, I am worse than a slave.' It is easy to complain and criticise God in our misfortunes, but some of the misfortunes can turn out to be our springboards for better things in the future. Joseph did not disparage God but continued to trust and rely on Him. So the prison became another stepping stone; another level of training for Joseph.

In prison the Lord was once again with Joseph and showed him mercy and gave him favour in the sight of the prison keeper. 'And the keeper of the prison committed to Joseph's hand all the prisoners who were in prison; whatever they did there, it was his doing. The keeper of the prison did not look into anything that was under Joseph's authority because the Lord was with him and whatever he did, the Lord made it prosper.' (Gen 39.22-23).

Joseph overcame his own needs and burden. He learnt the prison ethics and its economics so well that he was able to help other prisoners and supervise them. Despite the untrue accusation against him and his unfair judgment, Joseph's heart was healthy enough to help others who were depressed, abused, and rejected in the prison.

In prison Joseph met two prisoners of Pharaoh; one was the chief butler and the other was the chief baker. Both of them had dreams they didn't understand, so Joseph interpreted the dreams for them and asked the chief butler to make mention of him to Pharaoh when acquitted. The chief butler was to be acquitted and restored and the chief baker was to be hanged. Joseph's interpretation came exactly true. The chief butler was pardoned and restored to his job and the chief baker was hanged, but the chief butler forgot all about Joseph for two years. Joseph had to learn more about human nature and deal with rejection and disappointment.

For two years Joseph stayed in the prison incognito. He didn't know his future, but God was testing him and preparing him for his future assignment. The prison was referred to as a dungeon by KJV in Gen 40.15 and Gen 41.14. The Hebrew word for dungeon is *bor*. It means a pit or hole. Therefore, it was not a normal prison but a more severe prison, like a closed, deep, and dark cistern, where they normally would chain people. The Psalmist says, 'They hurt his feet with fetters, he was laid in iron. Until the time that his word came to pass, the word of God tested him. The king sent and released him, the ruler of the people let him go free. He made him the lord of his house and ruler of all his possessions, to bind his princes at his pleasure and teach the elders wisdom.' (Psa 105.18-22)

Pharaoh had a dream which no one could interpret. The chief butler then remembered Joseph and they brought him quickly out of the dungeon, and he shaved, changed his clothing, and came to

Pharaoh. The grace of God was upon Joseph and God gave him the interpretation of the dream. The interpretation of Pharaoh's dream was that there were going to come seven years of great plenty throughout all the land of Egypt, but after that would come 'seven years of famine,' so severe that all the years of plenty would be forgotten and the land would be depleted (Gen 41.30-31). He advised Pharaoh to select a discerning and wise man and set him over the land of Egypt and appoint officers to gather all the food of those good years that were coming, and store up grain under the authority of Pharaoh and use it as a reserve for the seven years of famine so that the land might not perish during the famine.

Pharaoh said to Joseph, 'Inasmuch as God has shown you all this, there is no one as discerning and wise as you. You shall be over my house, and all my people shall be ruled according to your word; only in regard to the throne will I be greater than you … See I have set you over all the land of Egypt … Then Pharaoh took his signet ring off his hand and put it on Joseph's hand and he clothed him in garments of fine linen and put a gold chain around his neck … and he had him ride in the second chariot which he had and they cried before him … So he set him over all the land of Egypt.' (Gen 41.39-43).

The brothers of Joseph took away his tunic, but they could not take away his destiny, because it was not in the tunic. The tunic was just a symbol of it. When the famine became severe in Canaan, Joseph's brothers went to Egypt to buy grain. Joseph recognised them but his brothers did not recognise him initially. When Joseph finally revealed himself to his brothers, he told them: 'I am Joseph your brother, whom you sold into Egypt. But now, do not therefore be grieved or angry with yourselves because you sold me here; for God sent me before you to preserve life … So now it was not you who sent me here, but God; and He has made me a father to Pharaoh and lord of all his house, and a ruler throughout all the land of Egypt.' (Gen 45.4-8).

Joseph sent for his father, Israel, and the family were given a land to settle in Egypt, not far from where Joseph lived in 'On.' 'All the persons who went with Jacob to Egypt, who came from his body, besides Jacob's sons' wives, were sixty-six persons in all. And the sons of Joseph who were born to him in Egypt were two persons. All the persons of the house of Jacob who went to Egypt were seventy.' (Gen 46.26-27). Joseph settled his family in the best land of Goshen and provided for their needs.

Joseph means 'let him add' or simply 'add' or 'increase,' but Pharaoh changed his name to Zaphnath-Paaneah, meaning 'Preserver of the age' in Coptic. 'And Pharaoh called Joseph's name Zaphnath-Paaneah. And he gave him as a wife, Asenath, the daughter of Poti-Pherah, priest of On. So Joseph went out over all the land of Egypt.' (Gen 41.45).

'On' was a city on the east bank of the Nile Delta. It was referred to as the city of Aven in Eze.30.17, as Beth-shemesh in Jer 43.13 and as Heliopolis in Greek. Aven means idolatry and Beth-shemesh means the 'house of the sun'. Heliopolis also means the city of the sun. The city On was the centre of sun worship, and a university city. Philosophers came to study under the priests of On, of which Poti-Pherah was the chief. The temple of the sun god was so important that it was served by the most learned priesthood of the land. Easton Dictionary states that in this 'university' Moses gained 'all the wisdom of the Egyptians.'

The city of On, in ancient times, was full of obelisks dedicated to the sun god. Smith Dictionary states that not only was the city of On the home of Joseph, but was the traditional place to which, his far-off namesake took Mary and the babe Jesus in the flight to Egypt. The same dictionary also states that two famous obelisks, 'Cleopatra's Needle,' which stood before this city were taken to Alexandra, by Augustus Caesar in 23 AD, from where one of them was removed to London and the other to the central

Park in New York. Easton Dictionary says that the one in London was erected on the Thames Embankment.

Psalm 105 states that one of the duties of Joseph was to 'teach his elders wisdom.' KJV uses senators instead of elders, pointing to older men or ancient men. So, Joseph taught the wise men of Pharaoh wisdom. The Hyksos kings brought to Egypt new knowledge and wisdom in medicine, art, astronomy, and mathematics, and also new technological knowhow. Joseph might have been very gifted by God to have been able to teach Pharaoh's wise men because there might have been a lot of renowned wise men, philosophers, and occultists among the elders.

By marrying Asenath, the daughter of Poti-Pherah, priest of On, Joseph could easily have been co-opted into the idolatry of the sun-worship, witchcraft, and the occultic practices that accompanied idolatry. You just cannot be married to the daughter of the chief wizard and be completely free. The fact that Joseph began to teach the elders of Egypt meant Joseph was spiritually positioned above them by God; that there was something about the God of Joseph that baffled the best philosophers. Remember Joseph was the only one who could interpret the dream of Pharaoh of all the elders, magicians, wizards, and sorcerers in Egypt. I believe that the coming of his father, Jacob, might have strengthened his hands against the powerful forces of idolatry. Jacob adopted the children of Joseph, Ephraim, and Manasseh, in other to free the lineage of Joseph from the curse of sun-worship and witchcraft.

Joseph began work immediately. In the first seven plentiful years, 'Joseph gathered very much grain, as much as the sand of the sea, until he stopped counting, for it was immeasurable.' (Gen 41.49). Soon the seven years of plenty ended and the seven years of famine began. 'The famine was in all lands but in Egypt there was bread.' 'So when the land of Egypt was famished the people cried to Pharaoh for bread. Then Pharaoh said to all the Egyptians, 'Go to Joseph; whatever he says to you, do...' So all countries came to Joseph in Egypt to buy grain because the famine was severe in all lands.' (Gen 41.55-57)

Joseph was working under Pharaoh, but he had given all power and authority to Joseph to give bread not only to Egypt but to the world. Those who came to buy didn't need to go to the king, but to Joseph. Does it sound familiar? 'I am the bread of life. He who comes to me shall never hunger, and he who believes in Me shall never thirst.' (Joh 6.35). Joseph was the type of the Redeemer, the 'Preserver of the Age' as his Egyptian name indicated.

'And Joseph gathered up all the money that was found in the land of Egypt and in the land of Canaan, for the grain which they bought; and Joseph brought the money into Pharaoh's house.' The famine affected the economic climate of Egypt in such a way that all profitable businesses failed. They spend the bulk of their money to buy food to survive. In the later years, about the fifth year of the famine, the money failed; they did not have money to buy food.

When the money failed in the land of Egypt and in the land of Canaan, all the Egyptians came to Joseph and said, 'give us bread, for why should we die in your presence? For the money has failed.' Then Joseph said, 'Give your livestock, and I will give you bread for your livestock, if the money is gone.' So they brought their livestock to Joseph, and Joseph gave them bread in exchange for the horses, the flocks, the cattle of the herds and for the donkey. Thus, he fed them with bread in exchange for all their livestock that year (Gen 47.15-17).

Joseph had taken all the money in the land for Pharaoh. Next, he took all the livestock in Egypt also for Pharaoh. Joseph did not work for himself, but everything he collected went to Pharaoh. Joseph was concentrating all the wealth of the land into the hands of Pharaoh. One of the questions some economists will ask today is, why didn't Joseph exchange their goods for money so that the people could reuse it as they chose? Why didn't Joseph put the money back into the economy?

When that year had ended, they came to him the next year and said to him, 'We will not hide from my lord that our money is gone; my lord also has our herds of livestock. There is nothing left in the sight of my lord but our bodies and our lands. Why should we die before your eyes, both we and our land? Buy us and our land for bread, and we and our land will be servants of Pharaoh; give us seed, that we may live and not die, that the land may not be desolate.' Then Joseph bought all the land of Egypt for Pharaoh; for every man of Egypt sold his field, because the famine was severe upon them. So the land became Pharaoh's (Gen 27.18-20).

Physical money is perhaps the last means of one's privacy and dependence. If money fails, there will no longer be any privacy. The use of credit cards and internet transactions are hastening the world into a cashless society. If money fails, what shall we use to pay for services, for food and for other necessities? The Egyptian money failed after seven years of severe famine, and they were ready to exchange themselves, their identity, and their freedom for food and become servants of Pharaoh. It is known that after the First World War, money failed and became worthless in Germany. When money fails, one's identity, freedom and life will be on the line. The same pattern will be repeated in the end time, during the time of Tribulation. 'He causes all both small and great, rich and poor, free and slave, to receive a mark on their right hand or on their foreheads, and that no one may buy or sell except one who has the mark of the name of the beast, or the number of his name (Rev 13.16-17).'

Joseph's economic model was first to build a kingdom economic structure. There was no parliament or political system to determine what should be done. In a kingdom, everything depends on the pleasure of the king. If the king is good and benevolent and loves the people, the economic system benefits the people. If not, the people suffer. Such supreme and sovereign power and authority of kingship may not be a good idea for man because of his weaknesses and self-interest, but with God it is different. God is a great King (Mal 1.14), the King of kings and the Lord of lords (Rev 17.14, Rev19.6). He is merciful, gracious, longsuffering, abounding in goodness and truth, keeping mercy for thousands…(Exo 34.5-7). Apostle John says, 'And we have known and believed the love that God has for us. God is love, and he who abides in love abides in God and God in him.' (1Joh 4.16). Therefore, there is no King like God and there is no kingdom like God's kingdom.

Joseph was bringing Egypt under the model of the kingdom of God, the kingdom of El Shaddai, the All-Sufficient God. Joseph, for a time, fed the whole world with grain. There was no way Joseph could store grain that would feed the whole world. I believe that he was able to do that because he brought Egypt under the model of the kingdom of God, which has no lack. Secondly, I see in what happened in Joseph's model a precursor of what is about to happen in the last days. In the last days, food, water, wealth, and other resources will be concentrated in the hands of the Pharaohs of the day. Thirdly, the failure of money in the days of Joseph should give us an indication that money will fail in the last days. When money fails, we shall need Saviours like Joseph, who will have the ability to invoke the sufficiency of the kingdom of God. 'And Saviours shall come to Mount Zion to judge the mountains of Esau, and the kingdom shall be the Lord's.' (Oba 1.21).

Microchips are now being put into human bodies in some countries for various reasons. It may sound good, reasonable, and technological advantageous but it is definitely a precursor of the 'mark and the name of the beast,' which shall be revealed in the last days. One of the things that money failure will do in the end times is that it will force people to wholly depend on God on one hand or submit to the antichrist (devil) on the other hand. Scripture confirms that, 'If anyone worships the beast and his image, and receives his mark on his forehead or on his hand, he himself shall also drink of the wine of the wrath of God, which is poured out full strength into the cup of His indignation. He shall be tormented with fire and brimstone in the presence of the holy angels and in the presence of the Lamb.' (Rev 14.9-11).

And for the people, he moved them into the cities, from one end of the borders of Egypt to the other end...then Joseph said to the people, 'Indeed I have bought you and your land this day for Pharaoh. Look, here is seed for you, and you shall sow the land. And it shall come to pass in the harvest that you shall give one-fifth to Pharaoh. Four-fifths shall be your own, as seed for the field and for your food, for those of your households and as food for your little ones.' So they said, 'You have saved our lives; let us find favour in the sight of my lord, and we will be Pharaoh's servants.' And Joseph made it a law over the land of Egypt to this day, that Pharaoh should have one-fifth, except for the land of the priests only, which did not become Pharaoh's (Gen 47.21-26).

In the kingdom of God, God is the source of life and everything. What anybody receives on the earth is given on lease and/or under the principle of stewardship or as a favour. Nobody really owns anything, not even his/her life. 'We brought nothing into this world, and it is certain we can carry nothing out.' (1Tim 6.7). In Egypt, God was also using Joseph to set a pattern of what would happen in the end time.

And Joseph died, all his brothers, and all that generation. But the children of Israel were fruitful and increased abundantly, multiplied, and grew exceedingly mighty; and the land was filled with them (Exo 1.6-7).

God's blessing of multiplication – that the seed of Abraham would be as the stars in the heavens and as the sand on the seashore – was being fulfilled. Egypt became a place of comfort, prosperity, and peace for the seed of Abraham. With the entry of the Hyksos, God changed the economic and the political climate of Egypt to fulfil His covenant with Abraham. After that the situation changed and the Hyksos Pharaohs were overthrown by the indigenous Egyptian Pharaohs. The new Pharaohs did not know Joseph or his accomplishments, nor did they respect the children of Israel.

Now there arose a new king over Egypt, who did not know Joseph. And He said to his people, 'Look, the people of the children of Israel are more and mightier than we; come, let us deal shrewdly with them, lest they multiply, and it happens, in the event of war, that they also join our enemies and fight against us, and so go out of the land.' (Exo 1.8-10).

The new Egyptian Pharaohs saw the children of Israel as a threat; another group of foreigners who could fight them and rule over them again. In dealing shrewdly or wisely with the children of Israel, they aimed to prevent them from multiplying, to weaken them physically and morally, make them poor and keep them as slaves to work for them. That was demonically controlled, considering the level of idolatry in Egypt.

As a result, they changed the laws of the land and charged the children of Israel with heavy taxes, and set taskmasters (overseers or princes of burden) over them, who forced them and afflicted them with heavy duties. They forced the children of Israel into bitter slavery. But the children of Israel continued to multiply, even under pressure, because of the covenant of God with Abraham.

Therefore, they set taskmasters over them to afflict them with their burdens, and they built for Pharaoh supply cities, Pithom and Raamses. But the more they afflicted them, the more they multiplied and grew. And they were in dread of the children of Israel. So, the Egyptians made the children of Israel serve with rigor (Ex 1.11-13).

As slaves, the children of Israel were ill-treated, afflicted, and put under hard bondage, so their lives were bitter. It was to break their spirits, rob them of everything they had, ruin their health, shorten their lives, and decrease their number. In a way it was to psychologically force the children of Israel to desert their way of life, be incorporated into Egypt as slaves, desert their Hebrew God and become worshippers of false gods. That was and is the Egyptian model.

'Then the king of Egypt spoke to the Hebrew midwives, 'When you do the duties of a midwife for the Hebrew women, if it is a son, then you shall kill him; but if it is a daughter, then she shall live.' But the midwives feared God and did not do as the king of Egypt commanded them, but saved the male children alive. So Pharaoh commanded the children of Israel to sacrifice their sons to the Nile god. 'Every son who is born you shall cast into the river and every daughter you shall save." (Ex 1.15-22).

Through Pharaoh, the devil was trying to destroy the seed of Abraham, to stop the word of God coming to pass. Through the seed of Abraham would come the Saviour who would save the world. 'Now to Abraham and his Seed were the promises made. He does not say, 'And to seeds', as of many, but as of one. 'And to your Seed', who is Christ.' (Gal 3.16). So the source of the whole attack upon the children of Israel was Satanic, to prevent the seed of the woman from coming forth.

It was in that period that Moses was born and adopted by the daughter of Pharaoh. So, Moses stayed in the palace of Pharaoh and attended the best schools and universities in Egypt. One day he visited his people and killed an Egyptian in support of one of the slaves. When this was discovered, he ran away to Midian and became a shepherd. After forty years in Midian, God met him on Mount Sinai and sent him back to Egypt to deliver the children of Israel from bondage.

God told Abraham that his children would be strangers in a land and be afflicted four hundred years (Gen 15.13). Abraham received the promise when he was 75 years old. 25 years later he gave birth to Isaac. 5 years later Isaac was weaned and scoffed at by Ishmael, so Ishmael and Hagar were sent away. Isaac was 60 years old when he bore Jacob (Gen 25.26) and Jacob was 130 years when he went to Egypt (Gen 47.9). It means that for 190 years (60+130) the children of Israel were not living in Egypt and not afflicted. However, the affliction of Isaac started 5 years after he was born. It brought it down the number to 185 years. So, the children of Israel might have lived 215 years (400–185) in Egypt.

The Bible also says that "Now the sojourn of the children of Israel who lived in Egypt was four hundred and thirty years. And it came to pass at the end of the four hundred and thirty years – on that very same day – it came to pass that all the armies of the Lord went out from the land of Egypt.' (Ex 12.40-41). Abraham was also a stranger for thirty years, from the time he went to live in Canaan when he was 75 years old to the time when Isaac was weaned (25+5). So, if we include Abraham in the calculation, the number of years they lived as strangers in a foreign land would be 430 years (25+60+130+215).

Chapter 3

Israel Encounters Jehovah

Moses went back to Egypt and met with his brother Aaron and the elders of Israel. They went to Pharaoh to tell him the command of Jehovah, to let the children of Israel go. Pharaoh and the Egyptians were idol worshippers. They did not know Jehovah, the God of the Hebrews, as the only and true living God. If even they had heard of Him, they thought of Him as just one of the gods. When Pharaoh heard the message of freedom and deliverance for the children of Israel, Pharaoh rejected and flatly refused to heed the command of Jehovah and even retaliated with more oppression of the children of Israel. God had previously warned Moses:

And I will harden Pharaoh's heart, and multiply My signs and My wonders in the land of Egypt. But Pharaoh will not heed you, so that I may lay My hand on Egypt and bring My armies and My people, the children of Israel, out of the land of Egypt by great judgements. And the Egyptians shall know that I am the Lord, when I stretch out My hand on Egypt and bring out the children of Israel from among them.
Exo 7.3-5

The signs and wonders were called plagues (Ex 9.14). The Hebrew word for plague, *maggephah*, means a blow, stroke, pestilence, plague, or slaughter. The plagues were afflictions of epidemic proportions which affected the Egyptians and posed serious threats to their lives and survival. The purpose of the plagues was to compel Pharaoh and the Egyptians to let the children of Israel go and to let them know that Jehovah, the God of the Hebrews, was the one and the only true God (Exo 7.4-5, Exo 7.14, Exo 9.14-15, Exo 10.2, Exo 18.11).

The plagues also made a distinction between the children of Israel and the Egyptians. Through them Jehovah demonstrated His power and authority in ways both Pharaoh and the Egyptians could not ignore His superiority over the gods of Egypt. In other words, He brought judgment on both the Egyptians and their gods. He showed the Egyptians the futility, powerlessness, and falsehood of their many gods (Exo 8.22-23, Exo 9.16, Exo 12.12).

In all there were ten plagues. In the fifth plague, a severe pestilence killed all the livestock in the fields (Ex 9.17). Only very little livestock remained. That plague started the economic decline of Egypt. In the seventh plague all the livestock, trees, and herbs in the fields throughout the land of Egypt were destroyed by hail, fire, and thunderstorms. But in the land of Goshen where the children of Israel lived, there was no hail (Exo 9.13-35). So, a major economic crisis developed in Egypt. In the tenth and final plague, the firstborn of every man and animal in Egypt died, but the firstborns of the children of Israel were not harmed. After that Pharaoh and the Egyptians allowed the children of Israel to leave with great wealth (Exo 12.29-33).

Seventy members of the family of Jacob went to live in Egypt at the time when Joseph was the Governor of Egypt. At the time of the exodus, there were about six hundred thousand men on foot, excluding the women and the children (Exo 12.37-38); so the children of Israel could be numbered conservatively about two million people at the time of the exodus. A mixed multitude went with them, and they went with their livestock. The Lord had told the children of Israel to request articles of silver, gold, and clothing from their Egyptian neighbours. 'And the Lord had given the people favour in the sight of the Egyptians, so that they granted them what they requested. Thus they plundered the Egyptians.' (Exo 12.35-38, Exo 11.2, Exo 3.22).

And Moses took the bones of Joseph with him, for he had placed the children of Israel under solemn oath, saying, 'God will surely

visit you, and you shall carry up my bones from here with you.'
Exo 13.19

While the bones of Joseph were still in Egypt, the economic model he established was still in place. But when his bones were taken from Egypt, his framework of the kingdom government and economic structure was also taken away from Egypt, and so the economic structure of Egypt was never the same again.

Under the presence of Jehovah, in the form of the pillar of cloud and the pillar of fire, the children of Israel went through the Red Sea on dry ground; through the wilderness of Shur, where Jehovah turned the bitter waters into sweet waters. They continued through the wilderness of Sin, where Jehovah began to feed the children of Israel with manna from heaven, and into the wilderness of Sinai. 'In the third month after the children of Israel had gone out of the land of Egypt, on the same day, they came to the wilderness of Sinai... So Israel camped there before the mountain.' (Exo 19.1-2).

Israel left Egypt on the fifteenth day of the first month, Nisan (Exo 12.2-7). The first day of the third month, as the Bible says, would have been the forty-fifth day. Mount Sinai was the same mountain where Moses first encountered Jehovah in the burning bush. Jehovah told Moses, 'And this shall be a sign to you that I have sent you; when you have brought the people out of Egypt, you shall serve God on this mountain.' (Exo 3.12). The first thing the children of Israel were required to do at Mount Sinai when they came before Jehovah was to serve Him. The Hebrew word to serve, *abad*, according to the Lexicon to the Old Testament, means to work, to labour, to toil, to be worked, to cause to work, to worship and/or to cause to worship. The initial request would have been first to worship Jehovah and then to honour Him by their works. Mount Sinai was the reference point of the children of Israel to their relationship with Jehovah God. Moses went up Mount Sinai to report back to Jehovah and Jehovah said unto him:

Thus you shall say to the house of Jacob and tell the children of Israel you have seen what I did to the Egyptians, and how I bore you on eagle's wings and brought you to Myself. Now therefore, if you will indeed obey My voice and keep my covenant, then you shall be a special treasure to me above all people, for the earth is mine. And you shall be to Me a kingdom of priests and a holy nation. These are the words that you should speak to the children of Israel.

Exo 19.5-6.

Jehovah was laying a bilateral proposal before the children of Israel. He had this proposal in mind before He instructed Moses to bring the children of Israel before Him. It was a conditional covenant between Jehovah and the children of Israel. The children of Israel would have to play their part and Jehovah would play His part. The main foundation of the covenant for Israel was obedience and faithfulness. If the children of Israel were obedient and faithful to Him, then God would make the children of Israel, first a treasure above all the people of the earth, second, a kingdom of priests and third, a holy nation.

The Hebrew word, *segoollaw,* translated as a 'special treasure,' had to do with property, possession, and wealth. It meant Jehovah would have Israel for Himself as His own prized possession. Jehovah would keep and hold and treasure Israel as a husband would do to his wife. So, an intimate relationship would be made between Jehovah and the children of Israel, such as in a marriage covenant. Therefore, the message God sent to the children of Israel could be seen as a 'marriage proposal.' Israel was to become a member of God's family, a reflection of God on earth, receiving special attention, having special endowment and special blessing than the rest of the people on the earth. Those privileges would come at a cost of obedience and faithfulness.

Secondly, if the children of Israel would obey God and keep the covenant, then God would make them a kingdom of priests. A priest is one who has access to God. As priests of Jehovah, the children of Israel would know God's word, God's will, God's ways, and the protocols of engagement with Him. They would be able to teach others about God, reveal God's word to the world, and bring people closer to God. The children of Israel were to be a kingdom of priests not only to themselves but to the whole world. Thus, they would become intermediaries or intercessors between God and mankind.

Thirdly, if the children of Israel would obey God and keep the covenant, then they would become a holy nation. Jehovah is holy and the source of all holiness. Hannah praised God and said, 'No one is holy like the Lord. For there is none besides You, nor is there any rock like our God.' (1Sam 2.2). Jehovah told Moses to inform the children of Israel, 'You shall be holy, for I the Lord your God am holy (Lev 19.2). Israel, therefore, had to relate to Jehovah in holiness. Jehovah, through His living word and covenant relationship would guide the children of Israel to live and walk in holiness. Through their holy living, the children of Israel would be distinguished from all the other nations.

Any time the children of Israel would disobey God's voice and break the covenant, they would cease to have that special or marriage relationship with God and be like any other nation. They would also cease to be holy. In such a case the children of Israel would invite the curses of the covenant upon themselves. Joshua warned the children of Israel, 'You cannot serve the Lord, for He is a holy God. He is a jealous God. He will not forgive your transgressions nor your sins.' (Jos 24.19).

It was the first time God had expressed such an outward love for any nation. 'I love you, will you marry me?' Jehovah would live together with Israel in a close and deep relationship and love her, protect her, care for her as one would treat a wife. Each of them would be able to enter the other's secret place, explore the deep recesses of each other's mind, emotions, intellect, and heart. Their relationship would also be so deep and joyful that it could be classed as divine intercourse or ecstasy. Jehovah and Israel would enjoy each other's company and receive the abundance and privileges of each other's company and property. This type of relationship between Jehovah and man requires a covenant of obedience and faithfulness on the part of man. There could never have been such a deep relationship between God and the children of Israel without such a covenant.

Moses came down the mountain, called the elders and the children of Israel and told them of God's 'marriage proposal'. And all the elders accepted the proposal: 'All that the Lord has spoken we will do.' The stage was then set for a contractual agreement or a prenuptial agreement between Jehovah and the children of Israel. Jehovah came down Himself to proclaim the summary of the contract, which we call the Ten Commandments. 'Behold I come to you in thick cloud, that the people may hear when I speak with you and believe you forever.' (Exo 19.9). On the 50th day after they left Egypt (Sinai Pentecost), God came down on Mount Sinai in His glory and spoke to the hearing of the children of Israel.

The whole contractual agreement, abbreviated as the Ten Commandments, was as follows (Ex 20.1-17):

1. You shall not have no other gods before me
2. You shall not make for yourself a carved image. You shall not bow down to them and serve them.
3. You shall not take the name of the Lord your God in vain.
4. Remember the Sabbath and keep it holy.
5. Honour your father and your mother.
6. You shall not murder.
7. You shall not commit adultery.
8. You shall not steal.
9. You shall not bear false witness against your neighbour.
10. You shall not covet.

Those were the direct words of God Himself. The Ten Commandments formed the basic structure and foundation for a closer union, integration or 'marriage' between Jehovah and the children of Israel and between God and man in general. The essence of these words does not change, they are eternal. Therefore, they apply to both the Old Testament and the New Testament saints. I will speak more about them later in Chapter Seven.

The children of Israel had seen and become familiar with the pillar of cloud and the pillar of fire above them in their journey to Mount Sinai, but when they saw the glory of God as He descended on Mount Sinai, they became afraid and drew back. 'The sight of the glory of the Lord was like a consuming fire on the top of the mountain in the eyes of the children of Israel.' (Exo 24.17). 'Now all the people witnessed the thunderings, the lightning flashes, the sound of the trumpet and the mountain smoking; and when the people saw it, they trembled and stood afar off. Then they said to Moses, 'You speak with us. And we will hear; but let not God speak with us, lest we die." (Exo 20.18-19).

The children of Israel made Moses their mediator and would not go near God. Apostle Paul says that '...there is one God and one Mediator between God and men, the Man Christ Jesus.' (1Tim 2.5). So, Moses became a type of Christ and bridged the gap between Jehovah and the children of Israel. He told them, 'Do not fear, for God has come to test you and that His fear may be before you, so that you may not sin. So the people stood afar off, but Moses drew near the thick darkness where God was.' (Exo 20.20-21).

The fear of God Moses was referring to was founded on reverential fear; the awe of God's presence, awe of who He is and the awe of His power. Many believers can easily say that they love God but cannot or will hesitate to say that they fear Him because they have no experience of the awesome presence of God. The awesome display of God's glory which was meant to discourage the children of Israel from sin, did not stop the children of Israel from sinning. They either took Jehovah God for granted or the magnitude of God's glory drove them far from Him.

Moses went to the top of Mount Sinai several times to receive more details of the covenant and/or to take the responses of the children of Israel back to God. Part of the blessings of the covenant included:

1. Jehovah would be an enemy to their enemies and adversary to their adversaries and cut them off.
2. Jehovah would go before them and bring them to their destination.
3. Jehovah would bless their bread and their water.
4. He would take sickness away from the midst of them.
5. He would take miscarriage or barrenness from them.
6. He would send fear and cause confusion among all the people to whom they went.
7. He would make all their enemies turn their backs on them.
8. He would send hornets before them which would drive out the enemies, little by little until they have increased to inherit the land.
9. He would deliver the inhabitants into their hands.
10. He would drive them out before them.

(Exo 23.20-33)

All those promises were on condition of two things: obedience and faithfulness. God was sending a special angel, who had His name in Him, to go before the children of Israel. He warned them that the angel would not pardon their transgressions, so they should carefully obey Him. The curses connected with disobedience and unfaithfulness were spelt out in Deuteronomy chapter twenty-eight, verses fifteen to sixty-eight (Deu 28.15-68).

Jehovah God extended an invitation to the elders and the representatives of the people in keeping with the marriage ceremonies of the time. 'Come up to the Lord, you and Aaron, Nadab, Abihu and seventy Elders of Israel, and worship from afar, only Moses shall come near the Lord, but they shall not come near; nor shall the people go up with him.' (Exo 24.1-2).

Worship must be the first response when one comes before Jehovah God. The first time Moses met God, he was told not to draw near and to remove his sandals because the place he stood was holy ground (Exo 3.5). The same God later called Moses to draw near while the rest of the people, even Aaron, who later became the High Priest, were kept back. Moses had learnt to remove his sandals prophetically; he had learnt to deal with and deny the self and become sanctified by God's holy fire. The fire of God could no longer destroy him because there was no corruption or unholiness in him. In order words, God proclaimed Moses holy. Secondly, as a mediator of Israel, he acted as a priest, and he alone was permitted to stand before God on behalf of the children of Israel.

Moses came down from the mountain and told the people the details of the covenant. And the nation of Israel agreed again to obey it. 'All the words which the Lord has said we will do.' (Exo 24.3). Moses wrote all the words of the covenant and built an altar at the foot of the mountain with 12 pillars, symbolising the tribes of Israel. The children of Israel now had a written contract or covenant. He sent some young men to sacrifice burnt offering and peace offering to the Lord.

Moses took half of the blood in the basin and sprinkled it on the altar. Then he took the book of the Covenant and read it to the children of Israel. For the second time the children of Israel said, 'All that the Lord has said we will do and be obedient.' (Exo 24.7). Moses then took the other half of the blood and sprinkled the people and said, 'This is the blood of the covenant which the Lord has made with you according to all these words.' (Exo 24.8).

The 'marriage covenant' was ratified by blood. God was legally married to the nation of Israel. The marriage certificate had been signed. Aaron, Nadab, Abihu and seventy Elders of Israel honoured their invitation and went up the mountain to see God. They saw God, 'And there was under His feet as it were a paved work of sapphire stone, and it was like the very heavens in its clarity... So they saw God, and they ate and drank.' (Exo 24.10-11). The meal was also to seal and cement the marriage covenant, and their commitment to it.

Scripture confirms Jehovah as the husband of the nation of Israel. Prophet Isaiah says to Jerusalem, 'For your Maker is your husband, the Lord of hosts is His name; and your Redeemer is the Holy One of Israel; He is called the God of the whole earth.' (Isa 54.5). Jehovah Himself told the Israelites, 'Return, O backsliding children, says the Lord, for I am married to you...' (Jer 3.14). 'Behold the days are coming, says the Lord, when I will make a new covenant with the house of Israel and with the house of Judah – not according to the covenant that I made with their fathers in the day that I took them by the hand to lead them out of the land of Egypt, My covenant which they broke, though I was a husband to them, says the Lord.' (Jer 31.31-32).

The fruit of the 'covenant marriage' between Jehovah and the children of Israel was Christ. It was the only way the seed which God sowed in Abraham could grow and become flesh. When the marriage was ratified the incarnation of the seed of Christ became certain and mandatory. Therefore, if Israel were to break the covenant and reject God, they would also reject Christ, the anointed, and His ministry. That was what happened.

God called Moses up the mountain again to give him the tablets on which He had written the Ten Commandments. Before Moses went, he told the elders to wait until he came back and appointed Aaron and Hur to deputise for him. 'And he said to the elders, 'Wait here for us until we come back to you. Indeed,

Aaron and Hur are with you. If any man has a difficulty, let him go to them." (Exo 24.14). Moses took Joshua along and both of them walked into the cloud and waited on God.

For six days Moses and Joshua waited and prayed, but on the seventh day God called Moses alone out of the midst of the cloud to the top of the mountain. So, Moses went into the midst of the cloud, into the mountain, and was on the mountain forty days and forty nights (Exo 24.17-18). Once again, Joshua didn't go up any farther up the mountain, only Moses went and was enveloped by the cloud of consuming fire.

Chapter 4

The Golden Calf

Israel left Egypt on the 15th day of Nisan (March/April). Fifty days later (Sinai Pentecost), God descended on Mount Sinai in His glory and spoke the Ten Commandments to the hearing of the children of Israel. That day would have been the morning of the 6th of the third month, Sivan (May/June). The day after the Pentecost, Moses went up the mountain on God's instruction. 'Come up to Me on the mountain and be there; and I will give you tablets of stone, and the law and commandments which I have written, that you may teach them.' (Exo 24.12). Moses was on the mountain forty days and forty nights (Exo 24.16-18). If we include the six days Moses waited on the mountain with Joshua, the forty days and forty nights would have ended on the 17th of the fourth month, Tammuz (June/July).

On the 16th Tammuz, a day before Moses came down from the mountain, there was an incident in the camp of the children of Israel which provoked the anger of God. 'Now when the people saw that Moses delayed coming down from the mountain, the people gathered together to Aaron, and said to him, 'Come, make us gods that shall go before us, for as for this Moses, the man who brought us up out of the land of Egypt, we do not know what has become of him." (Exo 32.1).

Israel had just ratified a 'married covenant' with God. They had not even left the marriage grounds and could still see the glory of God on top of Mount Sinai. Nevertheless, they gathered themselves to Aaron and demanded for new gods to go before them. The Hebrew word used for gathered could also mean to gather for war. So, it was not just a peaceful gathering, but a rebellious gathering or an uprising. Some discontent might have started with few restless and impatient camp members and later swept through the camp as a rebellion.

The rebellion acquired a much stronger voice and became the voice of the people. 'We don't want Moses as our mediator anymore to lead us. We want the gods to lead us.' The voice of the people is not necessarily the voice of God and popular opinion may not necessarily be the will of God. In the same way, common beliefs, cultural norms, and democratic decisions may be good, but not necessarily of God.

Israel's marriage relationship with God placed her in the favour, blessing, and protection of God. It gave Israel dominion over all their neighbours and adversaries. Such a close relationship with God was a threat to the devil's plans. He would not sit down and watch the children of Israel take dominion over him. He would fight back, and he did. The devil will always try hard to break man's relationship with God.

The children of Israel had made Moses their mediator between them and Jehovah. If they had grown weary of Moses, why didn't they ask for another man but asked for the gods to lead them? Perhaps the children of Israel wanted gods they could see and touch. The children of Israel couldn't soon have forgotten how Moses stood before Pharaoh on their behalf and delivered them from their bitter bondage, how he led them through the Red Sea, how they ate and drank when there was no food and no water in the wilderness and how he gained victory over the Amalekites. Perhaps they thought that Moses was dead on the mountain or was delaying their progress to reaching the Promised Land. Whatever their reasons were, the children of Israel cast Moses, their mediator, aside as irrelevant in a very short time.

And Aaron said to them, 'Break off the golden earrings which are in the ears of your wives, your sons, and your daughters, and bring them to me.' It was not the custom of the Israelites to wear earrings, but among them were Egyptian converts and people from other nations. They also had articles of gold which they received from their Egyptian neighbours. Aaron of all people should have known that what the people were asking for was a great and grievous sin; that which would break their covenant with God.

Moses left behind two deputies, Aaron and Hur, when he went up the mountain (Exo 24.14). The identity of Hur and what happened to him is unclear, but not that of Aaron. Aaron was the senior brother of Moses. In Egypt, God used Aaron to bring judgement to the gods and he worked with Moses to perform mighty miracles. He was one of those invited up the mountain to see God. He saw God and ate in His presence as a representative of the people in connection with the ratification of their 'marriage covenant.' What happened to Aaron?

Why did Aaron oblige and grant the children of Israel their sinful request? If Aaron was afraid of the rebellious mob, then he chose to compromise the covenant to save his own life. The Bible does not give any indication that Aaron tried to object to their demands nor tried to discourage them from their quest. Where were the other Elders who saw God and dined in His presence? Where was Miriam and her song of victory? There are many unanswered questions. What I see is that a new unseen (demonic) master had taken over the camp.

When Aaron received the gold earrings, 'he fashioned it with the engraving tool, and made a moulded calf.' (Exo 32.4). Aaron most probably first made a mould of a calf and overlaid it with gold, or he poured liquid gold into a moulded container. The moulded calf was not made by accident. Aaron knew exactly what he was doing. He had a mental picture of it before it was made. The question we may ask is, why a calf? A calf is a young cow or bull, thought to have great strength, growth, and fertility potential.

The children of Israel when they saw the golden calf said, 'This is your god, O Israel that brought you out of the land of Egypt.' (Ex 32.4). The Hebrew word for God was *Elohim*. *Elohim* is the plural form of 'El' but translated as a singular noun for the supreme God by the Israelites and Christians. The plural form could also be used for judges, rulers, or magistrates. In both the Vine's Expository Dictionary and Strong's Dictionary and Lexicon, the name, *Elohim*, suggests strength, power, omnipotence, might and pre-eminence. *Elohim* is the Creator God who created the heavens and the earth. 'In the beginning God (Elohim) created the heavens and the earth.' (Gen 1.1). Elohim was the same Jehovah God whose glory was blazing on Mount Sinai, as a consuming fire in the sight of the children of Israel (Exo 24.17).

'This is your god'. The children of Israel spoke as if the golden calf was the physical symbol or representation of Jehovah God. Instead of the glory of the Almighty, omnipotent and incorruptible God, the children of Israel reduced and changed Him to the level of an animal, a cow or a bull which they had fashioned with their own hands. They did not want to completely abandon Him but associated or mixed Him with something they could see and touch. The problem was that God was holy, separated above all and could not be mixed with anything else. Jehovah Himself says, 'I am God, and there is no other; I am God and there is none like Me.' (Isa 46.9). The children of Israel blatantly broke the covenant God cut with them barely forty days ago.

Apostle Paul says, 'Professing to be wise, they became fools and changed the glory of the incorruptible God into the image made like a corruptible man – and birds, and four-footed animals and creeping things.' (Rom 1.22-23). The Greek word for corruptible is *phthartos*. It means decay, perishable or mortal. Incorruptible is that which is undecaying, imperishable and immortal. The Psalmist says:

They made a calf in Horeb, and worshipped the moulded image. Thus they changed their glory into the image of an ox that eats grass. They forgot God their Saviour who had done great things in Egypt, wondrous works in the land of Ham, awesome things by the Red Sea.

Psa 106.19-22.

Horeb is another name for Mount Sinai. By moulding the golden calf, bowing down before it and serving it, the children of Israel corrupted themselves. They changed their own image patterned after the image of God into the image of corruptible things made by human hands. The way the children of Israel readily accepted the golden calf pointed to the fact that they knew about the golden calf and in their hearts had desired to worship it.

So when Aaron saw it, he built an altar before it. And Aaron made a proclamation and said, 'Tomorrow is the feast of the Lord. Then they rose early on the next day, offered burnt offerings, and brought peace offerings; and the people sat down to eat and drink, and rose up to play.' (Exo 32.5-6).

An altar is where the spiritual and the physical, God and man, meet. It is the place where man communes with and become one with what and who he worships. Whatever or whoever one worships and serves, he/she becomes like it. The first Adam was created a spiritual being in the image and likeness of God. The likeness of God included His character, righteousness, and power. Adam worshipped and walked with God, but his nature changed when he fell. Thereafter, he took on the nature of his new master, the devil. The altar of Aaron was a counterfeit altar and the blood of their burnt offerings and peace offerings gave the children of Israel access and union with the god of the golden calf.

The children of Israel celebrated their first Passover in Egypt and their first Pentecost at the foot of Mount Sinai. Now what feast was Aaron referring to? He said, 'feast of the Lord,' referring to one of the feasts of Jehovah. The day would have been the 17th of

Tammuz, which was not one of the feasts of Jehovah; Aaron and the children of Israel created a false 'feast of the Lord.' Whenever one changes his/her god, one must also of necessity change his/her festivals and celebrations. It proved that Jehovah God was not the same god as the golden calf. An idol may look innocent, but behind every idol is a demonic entity.

The feasts of the Lord were not just feasts of celebration. They were the fixed times God kept appointments with His people (Lev 23). The feasts of the Lord were the shadows or the rehearsals of God's salvation plan for humanity through Jesus Christ. To change the 'feasts of the Lord' was therefore to change the will and the plans of God for the salvation of humanity and the ministry of Jesus Christ. That was a serious sin and the consequence for such a sin was always grievous.

The children of Israel rose early the next day, 17th Tammuz, and offered voluntary burnt offerings, and peace offerings to their new god. The Hebrew word for the burnt sacrifice is *olah*. It means to ascend, to step up or to go up. It was a means of approach and union with their god. The blood of the burnt offerings and the peace offerings made the altar an interface between them and their god.

The Hebrew word for peace offering is *shelem*. It means requital, retribution, remuneration or reward. It was a voluntary sacrificial offering to give thanks for the goodness of their god or a sacrificial offering in the time of distress. The peace offering could also have been a vow of obedience or faithfulness (Lev 7.11-12, Lev 7.16). Not only did the children of Israel attribute their deliverance and all their blessings to the golden calf, they also committed themselves to being obedient and faithful to the god of the golden calf.

The children of Israel also 'sat down to eat and drink, and rose up to play.' They sealed their new-found union with the golden calf with a celebratory meal and drink. The Hebrew word for play is *tsachaq*. It means to laugh, mock, play, dance, make a sport of or make a toy of. The same word was used by Potiphar's wife to indicate that Joseph had tried to sexually assault her (Gen 39.14). So the phrase, 'rose up to play' suggested acts of a sexual nature; licentious or immoral sexual activity, free for all sex or sexual orgies. The children of Israel were treating sexual intercourse as a laughing matter, a plaything or something to make sport of.

Jehovah God informed Moses on the mountain top what was going on in the camp of the children of Israel and told him to go down. 'Go, get down! For your people whom you brought out of the land of Egypt have corrupted themselves. They have turned aside quickly out of the way which I commanded them. They have made themselves a moulded calf, and worshipped it and sacrificed to it, and said, 'This is your god, O Israel, that brought you out of the land of Egypt... Now therefore, let Me alone, that My wrath may burn hot against them and I may consume them. And I will make of you a great nation.' (Exo 32.7-10, Deu 9.12). Then Moses pleaded with Jehovah God (Exo 32.11-14). Before we deal with that let us first try to understand what the golden calf means.

Chapter 5

Myths Vs Beliefs

What did the golden calf at the foot of Mount Sinai symbolise? What god did the children of Israel mould to go before them? Who did the children of Israel worship and serve at the foot of Mount Sinai right before the glory of Jehovah God? What idolatrous worship was so significant as to contest with the worship of Jehovah God? Moses said, 'For their rock is not our Rock, even our enemies themselves being judges.' (Deu 32.31). We know that the Rock of the children of Israel was Jehovah God. What was the new rock at the foot of the mountain? Let's find out.

The children of Israel had just come out of Egypt. Egypt was polytheistic and worshipped many gods and goddesses. The children of Israel had seen the Egyptians worship the god of the Nile, god of the sky, of heaven, land, rainfall, fertility, love, war, and many others. One of the gods the Egyptians worshipped was Ptah. Ptah was a principal Egyptian god, a creator god represented by a live bull, called Apis (api, hapi, hep). Ptah was thought to be one of the sons of God (El) dwelling in Memphis, Egypt. He was supposed to be the source of life and connected with the fertility of grains and herds. Ptah was also known to be the god and patron of wisdom and craftsmanship.

Originally Apis, Ptah's representative, mediator, or incarnate on earth was a fertility god worshipped in Memphis, but later Apis became the god of strength and power to many cities in Egypt. Apis was the most important of all the sacred animals in Egypt and was referred to as the 'renewal of life.' Sometimes, it was depicted as a bull with a sun disk between its horns.

Even though the children of Israel knew about Apis while in Egypt and might have participated in the worship of Apis, I don't think the golden calf moulded by Aaron in the wilderness was the symbol of Apis. The children of Israel had in their possession live bulls, but they chose to mould a golden calf instead of commissioning a sacred live bull. In the wilderness of Sinai, the children of Israel could still remember how Jehovah through Moses judged all the gods of Egypt and made them powerless, so I don't think the golden calf symbolised the gods in Egypt.

The children of Israel could still remember how Jehovah God opened the Red Sea for them to walk on dry land, how He gave them bread from heaven and water from the rock and how He fought their battles for them. The children of Israel knew the might of Jehovah God. They might have thought that if they replaced Moses with the golden calf, they would have a more powerful witness of Jehovah God in their midst. In other words, they would have more access to Jehovah God and procure more benefits and more blessings. If that was their thinking, then they had misunderstood the covenant they had just cut with Jehovah God.

The children of Israel had known about the myths and the beliefs of the Canaanites, the people living in the promise land, since the days of Abraham and Lot. The myths and/or the beliefs of the Canaanites were ripe during all the developmental stages of the children of Israel before their migration to Egypt. Therefore, they lived with both the myths and the beliefs of the Canaanite gods and the tenets and beliefs of the God of Abraham, Isaac, and Jacob, during that period. It was not unusual for the children of Israel to worship Jehovah God mixed with the worship of the Canaanite gods. In Egypt, despite their oppression, the children of Israel held on to their beliefs. The covenant Jehovah God cut with the children of Israel was meant to shape their lives to conform them into the image and likeness of Jehovah God and cut them off from the myths and the beliefs of the Canaanites, but it did not completely erase the myths and the beliefs of the Canaanites from their minds and hearts.

The archaeological discovery of the Ugaritic texts (Ras Shamra tablets) at Ugarit in 1928 revealed important myths and beliefs of the Canaanite religion, even during the days of Abraham and Lot. Noah had three sons, Shem, Ham and Japheth. Canaan, the fourth son of Ham, was cursed by Noah, his grandfather, because of the sins of his father, Ham. Canaan became the father of the Canaanites, whose land was promised to the children of Israel, the descendants of Shem. The Canaanites were so sinful and practised many abominable things that God instructed the children of Israel to destroy them and their gods completely, to have no covenant with them and not to intermarry with them (Deu 7.1-3). The Ten Commandments were given to the children of Israel in part to counteract the practices and the worship of the Canaanite gods.

In the mythology of Canaanite pantheon, the head- or father-god was called El (god). He was the father of the gods, the god of humanity and the god of wisdom. The name El is sometimes used as a generic name for deity or god. He was normally pictured seated on a throne or as a young bull. The strength and the virility of a young bull was the symbol of the god. So, the golden calf moulded by Aaron perfectly matched the symbolism of the Canaanite El. The plural of El is Elohim (gods), but is translated as a singular God for the Jehovah God of the Hebrews and the Christians (Gen 1.1). The children of Israel, therefore, might have mixed things up and assumed that the Canaanite El was the same as the Hebrew El (Elohim).

The El of the Canaanites and El of the Hebrews were not the same. The children of Israel might have been muddled in their minds and hearts but to physically mould a golden calf was to break the covenant Jehovah God made with them. 'You shall not make for yourself a carved image – any likeness of anything that is in heaven

74

above, or that is in the earth beneath, or that is in the water under the earth; you shall not bow down to them nor serve them. For I, the Lord your God, am a jealous God...' (Exo 20.4-5).

In the Canaanite mythology, El had a wife called Asherah. The plural of Asherah is Asherim and is translated as 'groves' in the Bible (Exo 34.13, Deu 7.5, Deu 12.3). In human form Asherah was symbolised by a nude woman with protruding breasts. She was also supposed to be the tree of life and therefore was also symbolised by a tree, or a pole. Asherah was the mother goddess, goddess of fertility and love. She became one of the consorts of her son, Baal. She was normally worshipped by a sacred pole or tree near Baal's temple at high places (Jud 6.25, 2 Kin 21.3). The high places were places of elevation, like hills or mountains, where temples and altars were erected for worship.

According to the Canaanite mythology, El and Asherah had seventy children. All the seventy children were gods, but the most important of them were Baal (Haddad), the male god of fertility; Yam, the god of the sea; and Mot, the god of death and sterility. There were twin daughters, Anath and Ashtoreth, who featured prominently in the mythology. Anath (Anat) was the goddess of love and war and a consort of Baal, and Ashtoreth was the goddess of lust, lovemaking, beauty, sensuality, and military pomp. Ashtoreth is mentioned three times in the Bible as the tutelary goddess of the Sidonians (1Kin 11.5, 1Kin 11.33, 2Kin 23.13).

In some Canaanite lore, Baal's father was Dagon, and he (Baal) supplanted El and became the king, the ruler and lord of the gods in the pantheon. Baal was the executive arm of the pantheon; the most important, the most powerful, the most popular, the most celebrated and most worshipped. So, the golden calf moulded by the children of Israel at the foot of Mount Sinai was in reality a symbol of Baal.

Baal was usually symbolised by a human body with the head of a bull, having two horns to reflect its strength, virility, and power.

He was also simply symbolised by a bull, a ram, or a thunderbolt. Idols of Baal also occurred in many forms and shapes depending on their location or the nature of the attributes expressed. Baal was worshipped, not only in Canaan but in Egypt, Greece, Rome, and other places under different names. He was the Zeus of Greece, the Jupiter of Rome, the Bel of Babylon, the Chemosh of Moab, and the Molech/Milcom of Ammon.

All the mythological gods seemed to have all the human vices, frailties, and shortcomings. Among other vices were covetousness, envy and jealousy, adultery, fornication, incest, sodomy, and bestiality. They could be filled with wrath, become violent murderers and fight for position, wealth, and fame. A battle broke out between Baal, the god of storm, and Yam, the god of the sea, to determine who would rule the earth. With the help of Anath, his sister and mistress, Baal won the battle and was called the lord of the earth. As the lord of the earth, Baal became the source of life, the life-giver, and the sustainer of life on the earth.

After the victory of Baal, the myth revealed another epic battle between Baal, the life-giver and Mot, the god of the death and sterility. Mot was the twin brother of Sheol, the goddess of the afterlife, who ruled over the regions of the underworld. In that battle Baal was lured into the underworld and killed by Mot. At the death of Baal, the rainfall stopped, the streams and the rivers became dry, and the earth became unfruitful and desolate.

El, the father-god, and Anath organised a funeral ceremony for Baal. At the funeral ceremony El gashed himself until blood flowed freely from his body. Perhaps to bring life to the earth again. After the funeral ceremony, Anath went to the underworld and fought with Mot and killed him. She was then able to resurrect his brother-lover, Baal. With the resurrection of Baal, rainfall returned to the earth. The streams and the rivers became full and began to flow again. Drought and barrenness were eradicated, and the earth became fertile again.

Worshippers of Baal believed that during the time of drought and famine or even during autumn and the dry seasons, Baal was asleep or going on a journey. This gave a background to Prophet Elijah's encounter with the prophets of Baal and Asherah. Prophet Elijah mocked the prophets of Baal and Asherah, 'Cry aloud, for he is a god, either he is meditating, or he is busy, or he is on a journey or perhaps he is sleeping and must be awakened. So they cried aloud, and cut themselves, as was their custom, with knives and lances, until blood gushed out of them.' (1Ki 18.27).

In the Canaanite mythology, El was the father-god, the creator-god and the head of the Canaanite pantheon. In the Hebrew Scripture, Jehovah God also identified Himself with the name El and revealed Himself as Elohim, El Shaddai, El Elyon and El Roi. Many of Jehovah's servants and messengers have 'el' as part of their names eg. Mishael, the angel Gabriel, and archangel Michael. He is the Hebrew Creator God, the eternal life-source of everything (Gen 1), the I AM, the being of everything in the universe (Exo 3.14).

Baal was seen as a king, lord, and ruler. So was the Jehovah God. The psalmist says, 'Jehovah is King forever and ever,' (Psa 10.16a) and God Himself says, 'I am a great King.' (Mal 1.14). Jehovah is translated as Lord. Abraham calls Him, 'Adonai,' meaning Lord or Master, and Adonai Jehovah, the Lord God. (Gen 15.8, Gen 18.3).

Baal was supposed to be the god of storm and thunder. Jehovah was also the God of storm and flew upon the wings of the wind and of the clouds (Psa 18.10, Isa 19.1). Jehovah thunders from heaven and sends hailstones and coals of fire. When Jehovah God thunders, Baal is silent (Psa 18.13, Jos 10.11). Baal was supposed to be the god of fire. When Elijah confronted the prophets of Baal and Ashtoreth on Mount Carmel, Jehovah God came down as fire and Baal could not send down any fire (1 Kin 18.36-39).

Baal was supposed to be the god of the sky and of the earth, god of the earth and of fertility. Yet he was silent when Jehovah God shut out rainfall for three and half years in the days of Elijah. In the Hebrew Scripture Jehovah is the Possessor of heaven and the earth (Gen 14.19). 'The sea is His, for He made it; and His hands formed the dry land.' (Psa 95.5). Jehovah God controlled the dew of heaven and the fatness of the earth (Gen 27.28). Jehovah God brought judgement on all the gods of Egypt, including Ptah, creator god, Apis, fertility god, Geb, god of the earth and Osiris, god of the underworld and vegetation. (Exo 12.12, Num 33.4). They were all silent and impotent before Jehovah God.

Baal was supposed to be the god of justice and protection, but he could not protect the Canaanites from the hands of Jehovah God. Moses spoke thus of Jehovah God, 'There is no one like the God of Jeshurun, who rides the heavens to help you, and in His Excellency on the clouds. The eternal God is your refuge, and underneath are the everlasting arms; He will thrust out the enemy from before you, and will say, 'Destroy!'" (Deu 33.26-27). Jeshurun means an upright one, a symbolic name for Israel.

Though the Canaanite El was mixed up with the Hebrew El and the Canaanite Baal was mixed up the Hebrew Jehovah, it is clear that they are not the same. The concepts behind them were totally different. I have already mentioned that the mythological gods of Canaan like El and Baal revelled in all sorts of vices; covetousness, envy, jealousy, adultery, fornication, incest, sodomy, violence, wickedness, murders, and many more. But Jehovah God is righteous, holy and love. When he revealed His glory to Moses, He proclaimed His name. 'The Lord, the Lord God, merciful and gracious, longsuffering, and abounding in goodness and truth, keeping mercy for thousands, forgiving iniquity and transgression and sin, by no means clearing the guilty, visiting the iniquity of the fathers upon the children and the children's children to the third and the fourth generation.' (Exo 34.6-7).
Jehovah God therefore cannot condone or be touched with sin, evil and wickedness. He destroyed the whole world in the days

of Noah and in the days of Lot because of sin and idolatry. He caused the children of Israel to be dispossessed of the very land He had given them in covenant because they behaved like the nations they dispossessed. You can see that Baal was and is a counterfeit and a substitute god which prevents and turns people away from the true and living God.

In big temples of Baal vestments were worn (2 Kin 10.2), and in other high places the worshippers would be allowed to kiss Baal's idol where possible or they would kiss their own right hands in reverence and adoration to Baal (I Kin 19.18, Hos 13.2). On the altars the worshippers burnt incense to Baal, and they also offered the best produce, especially the first fruits of both plants and animals, silver and gold. (2 Kin 23.5, Jer 11.13, Hos 2.8). Scriptures also confirm that the people of Judah sacrificed human beings as burnt offerings on the altars of Baal.

They even sacrificed their sons and their daughters to demons, and shed innocent blood, the blood of their sons and daughters whom they sacrificed to idols of Canaan and the land was polluted with blood. Thus they were defiled by their own works, and played the harlot by their own deeds. Therefore, the wrath of God was kindled against His people, so He abhorred His own inheritance.

(Ps 106.37-40)

Because they have forsaken Me and made this an alien place, because they have burned incense in it to other gods whom neither they, their fathers, nor the kings of Judah have known, and have filled this place with the blood of the innocents (they have also built the high places of Baal, to burn their sons with fire for burnt offerings to Baal which I did not command or speak, nor did it come into My mind).

Jer 19.4-5.

Apart from the human burnt offerings to Baal, they also sacrificed human beings through the fires of Molech. God commanded the children of Israel even before they reached the promise land, "You shall not let any of your descendants pass through the fire of Molech, nor shall you profane the name of your God: I am the Lord."

(Lev 18.21)

Molech means king. He was the fire god of the Ammonites, the lord and master of Ammon. He was the Ammonite equivalent of Baal, moulded in brass to withstand heat. Its body, with a bull's head, was hollowed, and his hands were outstretched like a man to receive the sacrifices of children. When the fire in its body was red hot, the priest would put the children into the outstretched arms to roll down into the burning fire. Children were also made to pass through long columns of the idols of Molech blazing with fire. The children would die from the flames or from the heat. Sometimes Baal was built to serve in the same way as Molech.

And they built the high places of Baal which are in the Valley of the Son of Hinnom, to cause their sons and their daughters to pass through the fire of Molech which I did not command them, nor did it come into My mind that they should do this abomination, to cause Judah to sin.

(Jer 32.35.)

Prominent among the tenets of Baalism was the fertility cult. The cult members used their bodies in rites which attempted to facilitate the processes and the continuity of the fertility of plants, animals, and mankind. Those rites naturally involved some sort of sexual union. In the mythology of the Canaanites, Baal had sexual intercourse with Asherah, his mother, and Anath, his sister to guarantee fertility of plants, animals and humans. This belief gave license to the priests and the priestesses of Baalism to openly perform public sexual intercourse. It also prompted Baal worshippers to do the same. The priestesses were referred to as 'sacred prostitutes' and the other female participants, 'temple prostitutes.' So the worship of Baal involved open and free sexual intercourse. Not only that, but also open homosexual practices were common. These sexual immoralities were supposed to be offerings to Baal.

It was also common in Baalism to have common meals in which Baal, the priests, the priestesses and the worshippers were supposed to eat together. Wine was consumed in great quantity, which produced some drunken behaviours, demonic ecstatic behaviours or 'prophetic utterances.' Sometimes the wine was spiked to increase its potency. Baal worship also involved self-lacerations or bloodletting, as was witnessed on Mount Carmel when Prophet Elijah confronted the prophets of Baal and Ashtoreth.

Perhaps those licentious sexual practices and excessive eating and drinking, which satisfied the lusts, the desires, and the appetites of our baser human nature, were part of the great attraction to many worshippers of Baal, including the children of Israel. All humans, even of today, can have the same baser lusts and appetites, if they let themselves go. But such inordinate lusts, appetites and desires are not of God. Apostle Paul says, 'Do not be deceived, God is not mocked, for whatever a man sows, that he will also reap. For he who sows to his flesh will of the flesh reap corruption, but he who sows to the Spirit will of the Spirit reap everlasting life.' (Gal 6.7-8, also 1Joh 2.15-17).

Jehovah God as a righteous and holy God prohibited and condemned immoral sexual practices. In Leviticus chapter eighteen, He called the immoral sexual practices of the Canaanites wickedness, abomination and perversion and warned the children of Israel not to copy them.

Do not defile yourself with any of these things; for by all these the nations are defiled, which I am casting out before you, for the land is defiled; therefore I visit the punishment of its iniquity upon it, and the land vomits out its inhabitants.

(Lev 18.24-25)

One of the sins that defiled and still defiles a land or a nation is sexual immorality. In Leviticus chapter eighteen, God dealt with all types of sexual immorality, including incest, adultery, homosexuality, and bestiality. In verse six it says, 'None of you shall approach anyone who is near of kin to him, to uncover his nakedness.' Verse twenty goes on, 'You shall not lie carnally with your neighbour's wife, to defile yourself with her...You shall not lie with a male as with a woman. It is an abomination. Nor shall you mate with any animal to defile yourself with it. Nor shall any woman stand before an animal to mate with it. It is perversion.' (Lev 18.20, Lev 18.22-23).

You shall therefore keep My statutes and My judgments, and shall not commit any of these abominations, either any of your own nation or any stranger who dwells among you (for all these abominations the men of the land have done, who were before you, and thus the land is defiled), lest the land vomit you out also when you defile it, as it vomited out the nations that were before you.

(Lev 18.26-28)

Sexual relationship between same gender, such as between two men or two women is homosexuality. Sodomy can broadly be defined as sexual penetration aside from vaginal intercourse. It can cover both anal and oral intercourse. All homosexual men are sodomites, but not all sodomites are homosexuals. It means that married couple can run into the sin of sodomy without knowing it and incur God's wrath. Sexual intercourse between humans and animals is called bestiality.

Sexual intercourse with someone near of kin is incest and it is referred to as wickedness in the Bible (Lev 18.17, Lev 20.14). Both homosexuality and sodomy fall under God's hammer of 'abomination' while bestiality falls under the hammer of 'perversion' in the Bible (Lev 18.22-23). Abomination means that which is disgusting and abhorrent unto God. The Hebrew word for 'perversion' is *tehbel*. It means mixture, violation of natural and divine order. KJV uses the word 'confusion' instead of perversion. These are not my words, nor the words of man, but God's. It is God's standard of righteousness and not man's standard. Man can say what he/she wants and find reasons and arguments to support his/her actions, but it does not change God's standard of righteousness. If you want to walk with God, then you must also walk by His righteous standards.

All these acts of sexual wickedness, abomination and perversion were committed by the Canaanites. They were having sexual relationships with both mother and daughter and having sexual relationships with women in their customary period. They practised incest, adultery, fornication, human sacrifices, sodomy (homosexuality), and bestiality. All these were not uncommon among the Canaanites, as could be seen among the generation of Sodom and Gomorrah in the days of Abraham and Lot (Lev 18.6-23, Lev 20.10-21, Gen 19.1-8).

As a result of the immoral sexual practices, the Canaanites became nauseating to the land, and it vomited them out. In fact, when the sins of the Amorites (Canaanites) became full, God overthrew them and gave their land to the children of Israel. God warned the children of Israel that if they defiled themselves by the practices of the Canaanites, then the land would vomit them out and He would throw them out of the land (Lev 18.24-28). In fact, the same thing happened to the children of Israel. God threw them out of the land He had given them by covenant.

Baalism, through its fertility cult, opposed the sanctity of marriage between a man and a woman. The family unit as the fabric of human society and the nation was undermined by the flagrant abuse of sexual practices and human sacrifice. Women with unwanted pregnancies did not need abortion. They gave birth and offered their children for child sacrifices. So, child sacrifice was an alternative to abortion in those days. Some women were purposefully impregnated so that their children could be sacrificed to Baal.

The immoral sexual practices and the culture of the Canaanites were reflections of their gods. So, the immoral sexual practices were a form of worship to their gods. Attached to those gods or idols, in this case Baal, were/are powerful demons or demonic entities which controlled and perpetuated those practices. The Psalmist says, 'They even sacrificed their sons and their daughters to demons.' (Psa 106.37). Prophet Moses also said the same thing. 'They sacrificed to demons, not to God...' (Deu 32.17).

In the plains of Moab, just before the children of Israel reached the Promised Land, the king of Moab, Balak, sent for Balaam to come and curse the children of Israel. God did not allow him to curse the children of Israel. So, Balaam advised Balak to send their women into the camp of Israel to entice the men to commit fornication and incur the wrath of God (Num 31.16). The king followed the advice of Balaam, and the children of Israel committed sexual fornication with the women of Moab and the anger of the Lord was aroused against Israel. 'Now Israel remained in Acacia Grove, and the people began to commit harlotry with the women of Moab. They invited the people to the sacrifices of their gods, and the people ate and bowed down to their gods. So Israel was joined to Baal of Peor, and the anger of the Lord was aroused against Israel.' (Num 25.1-3). It was not just fornication, it was the union to Baal of Peor through sexual intercourse. In sexual intercourse the two become one (1Cor 6.15-17). God sent a plague against the children of Israel and 24,000 died.

Moses warned the children of Israel to destroy the Canaanites completely and not to have anything to do with them.

When the Lord your God brings you into the land which you go to possess, and has cast out many nations before you, the Hittites and the Girgashites and the Amorites and the Canaanites and the Perizzites and the Hivites and the Jebusites, seven nations greater and mightier that you, and when the Lord your God delivers them over to you, you shall conquer them and utterly destroy them. You shall make no covenant with them nor show mercy to them. Nor shall you make marriages with them. You shall not give your daughter to their son, nor take their daughter for your son. For they will turn your sons away from following Me, to serve other gods; so the anger of the Lord will be aroused against you and destroy you suddenly.

Deu 7.1-4.

You shall utterly destroy all the places where the nations which you shall dispossess served their gods, on the high mountains and on the hills and under every green tree. And you shall destroy their altars, break their sacred pillars, and burn their wooden images with fire; you shall cut down the carved images of their gods and destroy their names from that place. You shall not worship the Lord your God with such things.

Deu 12.2-4

Joshua led the children of Israel through the Jordan into the promise land and divided the Promised Land to the twelve tribes of Israel. In Joshua's farewell address he told the children of Israel. "Therefore take careful heed to yourselves, that you love the Lord your God. Or else, if indeed you do go back, and cling to the remnant of these nations – these that remain among you – and make marriages with them, and go in to them and they to you. Know for certain that the Lord your God will no longer drive out these nations from before you. But they shall be snares and traps to you, and scourges on your sides and thorns in your eyes, until you perish from this good land which the Lord you God has given you.

(Jos 23.11-13, Jud 2.1-3)

Joshua also admonished the children of Israel; 'Now therefore, fear the Lord, serve Him in sincerity and in truth, and put away the gods which your fathers served on the other side of the river and in Egypt. Serve the Lord! And if it seems evil to you to serve the Lord, choose for yourselves this day whom you will serve, whether the gods which your fathers served that were on the other side of the river, or the gods of the Amorites, in whose land you dwell. But as for me and my house, we will serve the Lord.'

(Jos 24.14-5).

Many of the tribes of Israel could not completely destroy or drive out the Canaanites as the Lord God instructed but lived with them. So the children of Israel were led to forsake their God several times to serve the Canaanite gods. 'Then the children of Israel did evil in the sight of the Lord, and they served Baals. And they forsook the Lord God of their fathers, who had brought them out of the land of Egypt and they followed other gods from among the gods of the people who were around them and they bowed down to them; and they provoked the Lord to anger. They forsook the Lord and served Baal and the Ashtoreths.' (Jud 2.11-12).

The Hebrew word for forsake, also means to loosen, to relinquish and to permit. It gives the impression that the children of Israel mixed the worship of Jehovah with the worship of Baal and Ashtoreths. They assumed that the worship of Baal would bring them more prosperity, and more blessings.

The anger of the Lord was hot against Israel, so he delivered them into the hands of plunderers who despoiled them; and He sold them into the hands of their enemies all around so that they could no longer stand before their enemies. Wherever they went out, the hand of the Lord was against them for calamity, as the Lord had said, and as the Lord had sworn to them. And they were greatly distressed (Jud 2.14-15).

Whenever the children of Israel cried to God, God would raise a judge for them. The judges were used by God to deliver the children of Israel from their enemies and oppressors. But the children of Israel would revert to worshipping Baal again after the death of the judges. 'And it came to pass, when the judge was dead, that they reverted and behaved corruptly than their fathers, by following other gods, to serve them and bow down to them. They did not cease from their own doings nor from their stubborn way.' (Jud 2.19, Jud 3.7-8). The last judge of Israel was Samuel. Then came the kingdom of Saul and the kingdoms of David and Solomon.

King Solomon, the son of David, started his kingship very well, pleasing the Lord God. However, King Solomon did not the heed the commandments of God and married many foreign wives, who turned his heart away from God to serve other gods (1Kin 11.2-3). 'For Solomon went after Ashtoreth the goddess of the Sidonians, and after Milcom the abomination of the Ammonites. Solomon did evil in the sight of the Lord, and did not fully follow the Lord, as his father David. Then Solomon built a high place for Chemosh the abomination of Moab, on the hill that is east of Jerusalem, and for Molech the abomination of the people of Ammon. And he did likewise for all his foreign wives, who burned incense and sacrificed to their gods.' (I Kin 115-8).

King Solomon's change of heart provoked the Lord God to anger so He tore away ten tribes of Israel from the kingdom after his death (1 Kin 11.11). The kingdom thus divided into two, the ten tribes of the northern kingdom, the house of Israel, and the two tribes of the southern kingdom, the house of Judah.

The first king of the northern kingdom was king Jeroboam. He set up two altars of golden calves in his kingdom and said to his people, 'It is too much for you to go up to Jerusalem. Here are your gods, O Israel, which brought you up from the land of Egypt.' And he set one in Bethel and the other he put in Dan.' (1Kin 12.28-29). The word used for gods is 'elohim'. The same word Aaron and the children of Israel used for the golden calf in the wilderness and the same word used for Jehovah God. King Jeroboam was not present at the foot of Mount Sinai when Israel sinned with the golden calf, but he echoed the same sentiments of Aaron. 'This is your god, O Israel that brought you out of the land of Egypt.'

King Jeroboam turned his people away from God because he was afraid that if his people went to Jerusalem to worship Jehovah, they would forsake him and serve Rehoboam, king of Judah. Therefore, he led his own people to forsake God. In doing so, he exposed the motives behind the worship of the golden calf; selfishness, greed, and profit. King Jeroboam changed the feasts days like Aaron and appointed priests who were not Levites (1 Kin 12-32-33). He himself officiated as a priest (1 Kin 13.33-34).

As I have mentioned, the feasts of the Lord were not just feasts but also pointers to God's redemption plan of humanity through Jesus Christ. Worshipping another god was bad enough, but changing the feasts was unpardonable because it sought to change God's redemption plan of humanity through Jesus Christ.

God pronounced judgement on King Jeroboam through prophet Ahijah. 'Therefore behold! I will bring disaster on the house of Jeroboam, and will cut off from Jeroboam every male in Israel, bond and free; I will take away the remnant of the house of Jeroboam, as one takes away refuse until it is all gone. The dogs shall eat whoever belongs to Jeroboam and dies in the city, and birds of the air shall eat whoever dies in the field; for the Lord has spoken.' (1 Kin 14.10-11). The golden calves changed the identity and the destiny of king Jeroboam and that of the northern kingdom of Israel.

The succeeding kings of the northern kingdom continued with the worship of the golden calves, so the house of Israel lived in perpetual sin. To them Jehovah God also pronounced judgement. 'For the Lord will strike Israel, as a reed is shaken in the water. He will uproot Israel from this good land which He gave to their fathers, and will scatter them beyond the river, because they have made their wooden images provoking the Lord to anger. And He will give Israel up because of the sins of Jeroboam, who sinned and who made Israel sin.' (1 Kin 14.15-16).

In the days of King Ahab of the house of Israel, the worship of Baal reached a point where the king, motivated by his wife, Jezebel, built an altar to Baal in the capital, Samaria, and sanctioned the worship of Baal as the official and national worship.

And it came to pass, as though it had been a trivial thing for him to walk in the sins of Jeroboam, the son of Nebat, that he took as wife Jezebel the daughter of Ethbaal, the king of the Sidonians; and he went and served Baal and worshipped him. Then he set up an altar for Baal in the temple of Baal, which he had built in Samaria.

(1 Kin 16.31-32)

The worship of the golden calf which started in the wilderness of Sinai had officially replaced the worship of Jehovah in Israel. The prophets of Baal and Asherah (or Ashtoreth) and their worshippers received governmental recognition and official support (1Kin 18.19), while the true prophets of Jehovah and the worshippers of Jehovah were hounded, persecuted, and murdered. The generation under King Ahab and wife Jezebel became an example of the golden calf generation; the worship of Baal and Asherah (or Ashtoreth).

The golden calf generation was met with the ministry of Prophet Elijah. Prophet Elijah confronted the Baal worship head-on. He asked the people, 'How long will you falter between two opinions? If the Lord is God follow Him; but if Baal, follow him.' (1 Kin 18.21). Elijah called the prophets of Baal and Asherah to a contest to prove which of the two was the true God. He overcame the prophets of Baal and Asherah, killed all the four hundred and fifty prophets of Baal.

The revival of Elijah was short-lived. Soon, the children of Israel fell back into Baalism again. It continued until the northern kingdom was overtaken by God's judgement. The Assyrians besieged the northern kingdom, Israel, took it and depopulated the northern kingdom. The King of Assyria sent people from other nations to live in the northern kingdom. Thus, the northern kingdom was no more and from that time, could not be identified.

After the demise of the northern kingdom, some of the kings of the southern kingdom followed suit. An example was King Ahaz. 'For he walked in the ways of the kings of Israel, and made moulded images for the Baals. He burned incense in the Valley of the Son of Hinnom and burned his children in the fire, according to the abomination of the nations whom the Lord had cast out before the children of Israel. And he sacrificed and burned incense on the high places, on the hills, and under every green tree.' (2 Chr 28.1-4).

Another example was King Manasseh, son of Hezekiah. King Manasseh rebuilt the high places his father, Hezekiah tore down. He built altars in the house of the Lord and served the host of heaven, the sun, the moon, and the stars in the courts of the temple. He sacrificed his children to Molech and shed innocent blood in Judah (2 Kin 21.2-8, 2 Kin 21.16). Manasseh, king of Judah, even did worse things than the Canaanites who originally defiled the land. King Manasseh was taken to Assyria, bound with bronze fetters, and carried to Babylon. When he repented the Lord brought him back to Jerusalem and he tried to undo the mess he had caused (2Chr 33.10-17). After his death, his son, King Amon, continued with the worst form of Baalism in the history of Judah (2Chr 33.11-20, 2 Chr 33.21.23).

The Lord God also pronounced judgement on Judah as He did on Samaria. 'Behold I am bringing such calamity upon Jerusalem and Judah, that whoever hears of it, both his ears will tingle. And I will stretch over Jerusalem the measuring line of Samaria and the plummet of the house of Ahab; I will wipe out Jerusalem as one wipes a dish, wiping it and turning it upside down. So I will forsake the remnant of My inheritance and deliver them into the hand of their enemies; and they shall become victims of plunder to all their enemies, because they have done evil in My sight and have provoked Me to anger since the day their fathers came out of Egypt, even to this day.' (2Kin 21.12-15).

Nebuchadnezzar, king of Babylon, besieged Jerusalem and took it in three phases. He destroyed the temple, the royal palace, and the city, and set them on fire in 586 BC. The prominent and many surviving people of Judah were deported to Babylon. Once again Jehovah judged His own people and carried them away from 'the land flowing with milk and honey.' He gave the children of Israel the land of Canaan in covenant. But because they did not obey His covenant but worshipped and served Baal, the god of the Canaanites and other foreign gods, He dispossessed them. The same or similar judgements will eventually befall any person, people or nation which would forsake God and worship and serve Baal and other gods. The cries of many prophets like Isaiah, Jeremiah, Ezekiel, Daniel, Joel, Hosea and Amos and Zechariah addressed the issue of idolatry but Israel did not listen to them.

Now that we have some idea about the golden calf Aaron set up at the foot of Mount Sinai, let us go back and see how Moses addressed the sin of the golden calf.

Chapter 6

The Priest Of Israel

And the Lord said to Moses on Mount Sinai, 'Go, get down! For your people whom you brought out of the land of Egypt have corrupted themselves.' (Exo 32.7). Moses, in his final review of the journey of the children of Israel in the wilderness, pointed to the urgency of the situation. 'Arise, go down quickly from here, for your people whom you brought out of Egypt have acted corruptly...' (Deu 9.12).

The Hebrew word, *shachath*, used for 'corrupted' means to ruin, decay, corrupt, mar, spoil or destroy. So, from God's perspective, the image and the identity of the children of Israel were tarnished, marred and ruined. The same Hebrew word was used to describe the earth and the people in the days of Noah. 'The earth was also corrupt before God, and the earth was filled with violence. So God looked upon the earth, and indeed it was corrupt, for all flesh had corrupted their way on the earth.' (Gen 6.11-12). The people in Noah's day first corrupted their hearts then filled the earth with wickedness and violence. 'Then the Lord saw that the wickedness of man was great in the earth, and that every intent of the thoughts of his hearts was only evil continually.' (Gen 6.5). In the same way, the children of Israel first corrupted their hearts before tarnishing and ruining themselves by moulding the golden calf.

From the time Moses met God in the burning bush He had always called the children of Israel 'My people.' But after they corrupted themselves with the golden calf, God said to Moses 'your people whom you brought out of the land of Egypt.' The sin of the golden calf had broken the covenant and wrecked the special (marriage) relationship between the children of Israel and God.

God continued with Moses, 'They have turned aside quickly out of the way which I commanded them. They have made themselves a moulded calf, and worshipped it and sacrificed to it, and said, 'This is your god, O Israel that brought you out of the land of Egypt!'' First the children of Israel made a moulded calf, then they worshipped it, then sacrificed to it and called it their god.

Just about six weeks earlier, the children of Israel had agreed to obey the commandments of God in a covenant relationship. The commandments formed the basis of the 'marriage covenant' between them. The breaking of the covenant wrecked their special relationship and communion with God and put a stumbling block to all the benefits and favours which came to them under the covenant.

God's first reaction to the sin of the golden calf was this. 'I have seen this people, and indeed it is a stiff-necked people! Now therefore, let Me alone, that My wrath may burn hot against them and I may consume them. And I will make of you a great nation.' (Exo 32.9-10). Moses recalled later, 'They provoked Him to jealousy with foreign gods; with abominations they provoked His anger. They sacrificed to demons, not to God, to gods they did not know, to new gods, new arrivals that your fathers did not fear.' (Deu 32.16-17).

God's initial reaction was to destroy the children of Israel and to start a new nation with Moses. However, God knew in advance that the children of Israel were difficult and stubborn people, yet He initiated and ratified a covenant with them. If God really wanted to consume the children of Israel, He would not need Moses' consent. What He said to Moses, 'let Me alone so that My wrath may burn hot against them' was to draw Moses out into intercession for his people, Israel. God first identified Moses with his people, 'Your people whom you brought out of the land of Egypt,' so that his intercession for them would be effective. Moses became not only the mediator for the children of

Israel but also the priest of Israel. Secondly, if God was going to raise a new nation out of Moses, then there would be no need to prompt Moses to intercede for his people.

Moses rose to the occasion as the priest of Israel and pleaded with God on behalf of Israel. 'Lord, why does Your wrath burn hot against Your people whom You have brought out of the land of Egypt with great power and with a mighty hand? Why should the Egyptians speak, and say, 'He brought them out to harm them, to kill them in the mountains and to consume them from the face of the earth'? Turn from Your fierce wrath, and relent from this harm to Your people. Remember Abraham, Isaac and Israel, Your servants, to whom You swore by Your own self, and said to them, 'I will multiply your descendants as the stars of the heaven; and all this land that I have spoken of I give to your descendants and they shall inherit it forever." (Exo 32.11-13).

This initial phase of Moses' priestly intercession was to tone down the fierce anger of Jehovah God and change His initial reaction. Moses reasoned with God that He should not destroy Israel for His own name's sake. First, the children of Israel were His people. Two, He brought them from Egypt with great demonstration of power before all people. Three, God would tarnish His own name and image and let people think that He intentionally brought them to Mount Sinai to destroy them. Four, He, God, had cut a blood covenant with Abraham, Isaac and Jacob for which He could not break.

If God were to break His covenant with Abraham, through whose seed the Messiah/Saviour of the world would come, He would have destroyed the eternal plan of salvation for mankind. The meeting of Melchizedek and Abraham would have been fruitless. To make a great nation of Moses would have been a great temptation to Moses if he was selfish and looking out for his own interest. But not Moses! He knew that Jehovah God was a covenant keeping God and he was just a servant appointed specifically for the fulfilment of His covenant with Abraham. It was impossible for God to break the blood covenant He cut with Abraham (Gen 15.9-16). Could it be that God was also testing Moses' heart?

God listened to Moses' plea and 'relented from the harm which He said He would do to His people' (Exo 32.14). Other versions use the word repent, 'And the Lord repented of the evil which He thought to do to His people.' God is free from sin, so He cannot repent. The Hebrew word used is *nacham*. It means to sign, by implication to be sorry, to console oneself, to repent, relent, to have compassion or to pity. So at Moses' initial intercession, God changed His intention, His mind and His conduct. He switched to His heart of compassion and pity and relented of His initial reaction.

Moses then turned from God and went down the mountain with the two tablets of the commandments engraved by the finger of God in his hands. He joined Joshua, who was on the lower mountain and both of them went down to the camp. Joshua initially thought that the noise coming from the camp was a noise of war, but Moses corrected him that it was the sound of singing. 'It is not the noise of the shout of victory, nor the noise of the cry of defeat, but the sound of singing I hear.' (Exo 32.18). The Hebrew word used for singing was *anah*. It means to afflict, to humble, to abase, to stoop, to defile or to exercise. It gave the impression that the singing was not solemn or sober but raucous and clamorous.

'So it was, as soon as he came near the camp, that he saw the calf and the dancing. So Moses' anger became hot, and he cast the tablets out of his hands and broke them at the foot of the mountain.' (Exo 32.19). On the broken tablets were engraved the Ten Commandments written by the finger of God. The Ten Commandments represented the moral law of God, which the children of Israel were to adhere to, in contrast to the moral decadence of the Canaanites. Obedience to the commandments would distinguish the children of Israel as a priestly nation, a holy nation and as the people of God. So the Ten Commandments pointed to who God was, His righteousness and His nature. They embodied the image and the likeness of Jehovah God. However, the children of Israel had already chosen the image and likeness of another god they would like to serve and be transformed into. The tablets with the Ten Commandments laid broken before the children of Israel. They did not need the Ten Commandments.

'Then he took the calf which they had made, burned it in the fire, and ground it to powder; and he scattered it on the water and made the children of Israel drink it.' (Exo 32.20). The sin committed by the children of Israel was the sin of adultery. They were unfaithful to their husband. 'Surely, as a wife treacherously departs from her husband, so you have dealt treacherously with Me, O house of Israel.' (Jer 3.20). So let's look briefly at the law of God concerning adultery. 'The man who commits adultery with another man's wife, he who commits adultery with his neighbour's wife, the adulterer and the adulteress, shall surely be put to death.' (Lev 20.10). According to the law of God both the idol, the golden calf and the children of Israel should be put to death.

Technically, the whole nation of Israel committed the adultery. But was everyone truly involved in that adultery? No! Then the law of jealousy must also be applied to find those who committed the adultery and put them to death. The law of jealousy says:

If any man's wife goes astray and behaves unfaithfully towards him, and the man lies with her carnally, and it is hidden from the eyes of the husband, and it is concealed that she has defiled herself, and there was no witness against her, nor was she caught – if the spirit of jealousy comes upon him and he becomes jealous of the wife, although she has not defiled herself – then the man shall bring his wife to the priest. He shall bring an offering... The priest shall take holy water in an earthen vessel, and take some of the dust that is on the floor of the tabernacle and

put it into the water. Then the priest shall stand the woman before the Lord, uncover the woman's head, and put the offering
for remembrance in her hands... And the priest shall have in his
hand the bitter water that brings a curse. And the priest shall
put the woman under oath, and say to the woman, 'If no man
has lain with you, and you have not gone astray to uncleanness
while under your husband's authority, be free from this bitter
water that brings a curse. But if you have gone astray while under your husband's authority, and if you have defied yourself and
some man other than your husband has lain with you,' – then
the priest shall put the woman under the oath of the curse, and
he shall say to the woman – 'the Lord make you a curse and an
oath among your people, when the Lord makes your thigh rot
and your belly swell and may this water that causes the curse go
into your stomach, and make your body swell and your thigh
rot...' Then the priest shall write these curses in a book, and he
shall scrape them off into the bitter water. And he shall make the
woman drink the bitter water that brings a curse, and the water
that brings the curse shall enter her to become bitter... When he
has made her drink the water, then it shall be, if she has defiled
herself and behaved unfaithfully towards her husband, that the
water that brings a curse will enter her and become bitter, and
her belly will swell, her thigh will rot, and the woman will be a
curse among her people. But if the woman has not defiled herself, and is clean, then she shall be free and may conceive children.

(Num 5.11-28)

The Bible says that Moses 'took the golden calf which Israel had
made, burned it in the fire, and ground it to powder; and he
scattered it on the water and made the children of Israel drink
it.' The Bible does not tell us how Moses burnt the golden calf,
and ground it like powder; but why did Moses go through all
that trouble in the first place? I believe that Moses was applying the law of jealousy on behalf of God. God had told the children of Israel that He was a Jealous God (Exo 20.5, Exo 34.14).

Those who were actually involved in that adultery must be separated out first and punished before reconciliation and repentance could be effective.

After Moses made the people drink the bitter suspension of gold and water, he then turned to Aaron. 'What did the people do to you that you have brought so great a sin upon them?' Aaron blamed the people and said when they brought the gold earrings he cast it into the fire and the calf came out. The question is why did he tell them to bring the gold if he did not know what he was going to do? It was also impossible for the golden calf to walk out from the fire. Aaron lied to defend himself. He knew exactly what he was doing. The question, 'What did the people do to Aaron?' was not answered. Perhaps Aaron repented of his heinous sin, but Scripture does not mention it. And up to that time nobody had repented of that sin, not even Moses.

Now when Moses saw that the people were unrestrained (for Aaron had not restrained them, to their shame among their enemies), then Moses stood in the entrance of the camp, and said, 'Whoever is on the Lord's side – come to me!' And all the sons of Levi gathered themselves together to him.

(Exo 32.25-26).

Moses, after applying the law of jealousy, began to see the true situation in the camp; that the people were lawless, under the control of the lawless one. Aaron had lost the power to lead them and bring order. The devil, the lawless one, had taken over the camp and the people were behaving in line with the character of the devil. It was time to separate those who had not corrupted themselves from those who had corrupted themselves. If not, the leaven of corruption would affect the whole camp.

Moses said to the sons of Levi, 'Thus says the Lord God of Israel: 'Let every man put his sword on his side, and go in and out from entrance to entrance throughout the camp, and let every man kill his brother, every man his companion, and every man his neighbour.' So the sons of Levi did according to the word of Moses. And about three thousand men of the people fell that day.' (Exo 32.27-28).

The census at the time of the exodus from Egypt was about six hundred thousand men (estimated about two million people altogether). That number was not any different at Mount Sinai. So how did the sons of Levi know whom to kill? I believe the bitter suspension of gold and water they had all drank brought into effect the law of jealousy. God relented on His decision to consume the whole nation, but He still consumed those who were actually involved in that adultery. As I said above, no atonement had up to that time been offered for the sin.

After the death of the three thousand people in the camp, Moses told the Levites to consecrate themselves to God for His service. 'Consecrate yourselves today to the Lord that He may bestow on you a blessing this day, for every man has opposed his son and his brother.' (Exo 32.29). It looks as if the Levites cleansed the camp of those corrupted irrespective of who they were; whether sons, brothers, or family members. Because of their zeal for the Lord God, the Levites were chosen for the service of God in the tabernacle.

Moses told the children of Israel, 'I stayed on the mountain forty days and forty nights. I neither ate bread nor drank water.' (Deu 9.9). The number forty is very significant in the Bible. In the flood judgement, it rained forty days and forty nights and every living thing died except Noah and his family (Gen 7.4.). Jesus fasted for forty days and forty nights before He started his earthly ministry (Mat 4.2, Luk.1-2). Elijah fasted forty days to meet with God for his next assignment (1Kin 19.8). After forty years in the wilderness Israel entered the Promised Land. Human pregnancy takes forty weeks. Forty is a time period which separates two major events. It is therefore a time of transition and change. Moses' stay of forty days and forty nights on Mount Sinai was the beginning of the time of transition from the old self-image of the children of Israel to the new image of God.

The coming down of Moses from the top of Mount Sinai was a picture and a type or shadow of the second coming of Jesus Christ. 'But in those days, after that tribulation, the sun will be darkened, and the moon will not give its light; the stars of heaven will fall, and the powers in the heavens will be shaken. Then they will see the Son of Man coming in the clouds with great power and glory.' 'Now I saw heaven opened, and behold, a white horse. And He who sat on him was called Faithful and True, and in righteousness He judges and makes war … And the armies in heaven clothed in fine linen, white and clean, followed Him on white horses.' (Rev 19.11-14, Mar 13.24-26, Mat 24.29-30, Luk 21.25-27).

At the end of His first earthly ministry, Jesus Christ ascended to heaven. As Jesus' disciples looked on when Jesus Christ ascended to heaven, two men in white apparel suddenly stood by them and said, 'Men of Galilee, why do you stand gazing up into heaven? This same Jesus, who was taken up from you into heaven, will so come in like manner as you saw Him go into heaven.' (Act 1.11).

Moses descended from Mount Sinai on 17th Tammuz. It was the same day that he broke the tablets of the Ten Commandments at the foot of the mountain. It is believed that 17th Tammuz was the same date in which the Babylonians breached the walls of Jerusalem to destroy the first temple. The same date, 17th Tammuz, was also believed to be the same date in which the Roman army breached the walls of Jerusalem to destroy the second temple. In Jewish tradition, 17th Tammuz begins a three-week fast known as Shivah Asar B'Tammuz to mourn for these events in their history.

Moses knew about the idolatry in the camp of Israel because God told him. He pleaded with God to change His mind about His initial anger and reaction. So Moses' own anger should not have been that hot; but when Moses saw the singing and the dancing in the camp, his own anger became so hot that he cast the tablets out of his hands and broke them at the foot of the mountain. What did Moses see that made his anger become so hot? He saw the golden calf openly displayed and a loud and boisterous partying and festive celebration to honour the Canaanite god of Baal. The Bible does not tell us, but it might have been some provocative, immoral, unrestrained, and licentious singing and dancing common with idolatrous worship.

Before the return of our Lord Jesus Christ, there will be a generation who will turn away from God to Baalism. This generation will behave in a licentious, immoral, unrestrained, and sexually provocative manner, such as the generation of the children of Israel Moses saw when he came down from the mountain. The Ten Commandments, God's image and likeness, will lay broken before this generation. They will worship and serve Baal and other gods. This generation will be the golden calf generation. When this golden calf generation becomes established, it will be a sign that the return of Jesus Christ is imminent and is very close. Now, let's get back to Moses in the camp of that golden calf generation.

Now it came to pass on the next day that Moses said to the people, 'You have committed a great sin. So now I will go up to the Lord; perhaps I can make atonement for your sin. Then Moses returned to the Lord and said, 'Oh, these people have committed a great sin, and have made for themselves a god of gold! Yet now, if You will forgive their sin – but if not, I pray, blot me out of Your book which You have written.' (Exo 32.31-32).

The next day was 18th Tammuz. Moses went back to the Lord God on the mountain with the main purpose of making atonement for the sin of Israel. He first confessed the sin of the children of Israel before God. The Bible does not complete Moses' full supplication, but it is obvious that Moses was pleading with God to forgive the sin of the nation of Israel. Even though those who were actively involved in the sin were dead, the whole nation still bore the sin of the golden calf. The whole nation had condoned them, shared in them, and become the golden calf generation. This also emphasises the fact that God did not really forgive Israel when Moses pleaded with Him not to destroy them. God just relented not to destroy them then.

The intercession of Moses might have been a difficult one. However, Moses put his own life on the line as well. 'Yet now, if You will forgive their sin – but if not, I pray, blot me out of Your book which You have written.' 'If it is not in Thy will to forgive them then blot me out of Your book instead.' This book of God in heaven contained the register of all the righteous, living or dead (Psa 69.28, Isa 4.3, Rev 3.5). If it was not the will of God to forgive the sin of the children of Israel, Moses was requesting God that His judgement should fall upon him instead. His name should be removed from the book of the righteous.

Now the true priestly intercession for the sin of the children of Israel had begun. Moses identified himself with his people. He was innocent but he offered himself to be judged in their place as the one who committed the sins. This is the basis for a priestly intercession and the basis for atonement; the sacrifice of the innocent. You enter the throne room of God and put your life down between God and the offender. That was the highest role of priestly intercession.

Apostle Paul had a similar supposition; 'For I could wish that I myself were accursed from Christ for my brethren, my countrymen according to the flesh.' (Rom 9.3).

In such a role, Moses became the type of our Lord Jesus Christ, our High Priest. 'Not with the blood of goats and calves but with His own blood He entered the Most Holy Place once for all, having obtained eternal redemption.' (Heb 9.12). Moses went to God to seek atonement; peace and reconciliation between God and the nation of Israel, not with goats and calves, but with himself as the substitute. He placed himself on the altar, presenting himself as a living sacrifice.

God replied to Moses: 'Whoever has sinned against Me, I will blot him out of My book. Now therefore, go, lead the people to the place of which I have spoken to you. Behold, My angel shall go before you. Nevertheless, in the day when I visit for punishment, I will visit punishment upon them for their sin.' So the Lord plagued the people because of what they did with the calf which Aaron made.' (Exo 32.33-35). God relented to not destroy the children of Israel, but His chastising hand remained on them for a long time.

The Bible gives an indication that Moses stayed up the mountain forty days and forty nights again without food and drinks. 'And I fell down before the Lord, as at first, forty days and forty nights; I neither ate bread nor drank water because of all your sin which you committed in doing wickedly in the sight of the Lord, to provoke Him to anger. For I was afraid of the anger and hot displeasure with which the Lord was angry with you to destroy you. But the Lord listened to me at that time also.' (Deu 9.18-19). Moses was not only willing to substitute his life for his people, he also didn't eat and drink for another forty days and forty nights, pleading for God's mercy on Israel.

God told Moses, 'Depart and go up from here, you and the people whom you have brought out of the land of Egypt, to the land of which I swore to Abraham, Isaac and Jacob, saying, 'To your descendants I will give it'. And I will send My angel before you … I will not go up in your midst, lest I consume you on the way, for you are a stiff-necked people.' (Exo 33.1-3). In the past, God's presence had gone before His people in the pillar of cloud and the pillar of fire. God told Moses that His Presence would not go with them because of the sin of the golden calf, but He would send His angel to go before them.

Moses returned to the camp on the 29th Av (July/August), but he did not give up. He pitched a tent outside the camp of Israel and called it the tabernacle of meeting. He continued to minister to the people, pleading and wrestling with God for the complete restoration of his people until God restored His very presence in the midst of Israel on account of Moses. 'My Presence will go with you, and I will give you rest.' Then he said to Him, 'If your Presence does not go with us, do not bring us up from here. For how then will it be known that Your people and I have found grace in your sight, except You go with us? So we shall be separate, Your people and I, from all the people who are upon the face of the earth. ... I will also do this thing that you have spoken; for you have found grace in My sight, and I know you by name.' (Exo 33.14-17).

Moses then made another amazing request: 'Please show me Your glory.' Moses was the only man who saw a form of Jehovah and spoke with Him face to face. He had seen the manifest Presence of God many times. But he desired to see more than the form, more than the shadow and the similitude. He asked to see Jehovah without the form and without the cloud. He wanted to see His real face.

Jehovah did not completely refuse Moses but said, 'I will make all My goodness pass before you and I will proclaim the name of the Lord before you. I will be gracious to whom I will be gracious and I will have compassion on whom I will have compassion.' But He said, 'You cannot see My face, for no man can see my face and live.' (Ex 33.19-20).

God later told Moses to cut new tablets of stone and bring them on the mountain so that He could write on them the words that were on the first tablets which were broken. 'Cut two tablets of stone like the first ones, and I will write on these tablets the words that were on the first tablets which you broke. So be ready in the morning, and come up in the morning to Mount Sinai, and present yourself to Me there on the top of the mountain.' (Exo 34.1-2). Moses went up again up the mountain with the tablets and stayed forty days and forty nights, the third time.

Then the Lord said to Moses, 'Write these words, for according to the tenor of these words I have made a covenant with you and Israel. So he was there with the Lord, forty days and forty nights; he neither ate bread nor drink water. And He wrote on the tablets the words of the covenant, the Ten Commandments.' (Exo 34.27-28).

On the mountain Jehovah God showed Moses His glory by passing before him and proclaiming His full seven-fold name. 'The Lord, the Lord God, merciful and gracious, longsuffering, and abounding in goodness and truth, keeping mercy for thousands, forgiving iniquity and transgression and sin, by no means clearing the guilty, visiting the iniquity of the fathers upon the children and the children's children to the third and the fourth generation.' (Exo 34.6-7). Then Jehovah God renewed the covenant with Moses and the children of Israel and asked Moses to write it down in a book like the first one. That was the second written covenant for the children of Israel. Finally, Jehovah God wrote the Ten Commandments again on the tablets which Moses had fashioned and brought.

The first set of tablets which Moses broke, on which were written the Ten Commandments, were fashioned by God Himself and written with His own finger. God revealed that He intended to write His laws on human hearts and not on stones. 'I will put My laws in their mind and write them on their hearts; and I will be their God, and they shall be My people.' (Heb 8.10). In that case the two tablets of stone represented the human heart (the two chambers), as Apostle Paul confirmed. (2 Cor 3.3). So the first set of the tablets fashioned and written by the finger of God would mean that God was going to write His word on the hearts of His people alone, without their effort. In other words, God was going to transform His people by His word into His own image, likeness, and character without human effort. That first set of tablets was broken.

The second set of tablets were fashioned by Moses and was engraved with the Ten Commandments by the finger of God. Before God could write on the tablets of stone Moses had to fashion the two tablets of stone with an implement. This indicates that before God can write His law on man's heart, he/she needs to prepare his/her own heart with the help of the Spirit of God. Before God can transform us into His image and likeness, there is a work to be done on ourselves. Apostle Paul says, 'I beseech you therefore, brethren, by the mercies of God, that you present your bodies a living sacrifice, holy, acceptable to God, which is your reasonable service. And do not be conformed to this world, but be transformed by the renewing of your mind, that you may prove what is that good and acceptable and perfect will of God.' (Rom 12.1-2). By presenting the body as a living sacrifice, one has to live an unblemished and holy life and be a living death to oneself.

Many nominal and intellectual Christians believe in 'once saved, always saved.' I don't. I think the idea makes many Christians complacent and makes them believe that they can walk in sin and unforgiveness and still go to heaven and enjoy the kingdom of God without impunity. Jesus says, 'If anyone desires to come after Me, let him deny himself, and take up his cross daily and follow Me.' (Luk 9.23). The cross is a symbol of death. One has to die to self that he may gain Christ. (Phil 3.7-11). Jesus speaking to the dead church in Sardis said, 'He who overcomes shall be clothed in white garments, and I will not blot out his name from the Book of Life but will confess his name before My Father and before angels.' (Rev 3.5). It is possible to blot out one's name from the book of life, as indicated by Moses' priestly intercession on the mountain.

Apostle Paul reveals, 'But I discipline my body, and bring it into subjection, lest, when I have preached to others, I myself should become disqualified.' (1Cor 9.27). The Greek word for 'disqualified' also means rejected, castaway, not approved, worthless, unworthy, or unfit. This teaches us that one can begin the Christian journey well and lose it in the end. Apostle Paul again reveals that Christians are reconciled through the death of Jesus Christ in order to present them holy and blameless and above reproach in God's sight: 'If indeed they continue in the faith, grounded and steadfast, and are not moved away from the hope of the gospel which you heard.' (Col 1.23). In other words, 'those who endure to the end shall be saved.' (Mat 10.22, Mat 24.13). And those who don't endure to the end will not be saved. The end of one's Christian journey is crucial.

Apostle Peter also admonishes us, 'For if, after they have escaped the pollutions of the world through the knowledge of the Lord and Saviour Jesus Christ, they are again entangled in them and overcome, the latter end is worse for them than the beginning. For it would have been better for them not to have known the way of righteousness, than having known it, to turn from the holy commandments delivered to them. But it has happened to them according to the true proverb: 'A dog returns to his own vomit' and 'a sow, having washed, to her wallowing in the mire.'' (2 Pet 2.20-22).

Apostle John also tells us, 'Beloved, now we are children of God; and it has not yet been revealed what we shall be, but we know that when He is revealed, we shall be like Him, for we shall see Him as He is. And everyone who has this hope in Him purifies himself, just as He is pure.' (1 Joh 3.2-3). One cannot live in unrighteousness and corruption and hope to be transformed into the image and likeness of our Lord Jesus Christ. It is an impossibility, a fallacy.

Moses returned from his second forty days and forty nights on the 29 Av. He went to the mountain for the third forty days and forty nights on 1 Elul (August/September). He therefore would have returned on 10 Tishri. Tishri is the first month of the civil year and the seventh of the ecclesiastical year, usually in September/October. 10 Tishri is exactly the Day of Atonement.

So, on 10 Tishri, the Day of Atonement, Moses procured the full atonement and a renewed covenant between Jehovah God and the children of Israel. The feast of the Day of Atonement therefore commemorates the day Moses received full atonement for the sin of Israel and came back with a renewed covenant. Every year on the Day of Atonement, 10 Tishri, the high priest would go back to the manifest presence of Jehovah God for a fresh copy of the atonement and a renewal of the covenant. When Jesus Christ came to the earth, He took His own blood to the throne of Grace once and for all and obtained eternal atonement for all mankind. 'Not with the blood of goats and calves, but with His own blood He entered the Most Holy Place once for all, having obtained eternal redemption.' (Heb 9.12, Heb 7.27).

Now it was so, when Moses came down from Mount Sinai (and the two tablets of the Testimony were in Moses' hand when he came down from the mountain), that Moses did not know that the skin of his face shone while he talked with Him (Exo 34.29).

Moses had been in the glory of God and spoken to Jehovah God for one hundred and twenty days without food and drink. It was and is humanly impossible; so the glory of God sustained Moses in such a way that he didn't need food and drink. 'Man shall not live by bread alone; but man lives by every word that proceeds from the mouth of the Lord.' (Deu 8.3, Mat 4.4, Luk 4.4). The glory of God also transformed his appearance to look like God. The children of Israel could not look steadily at Moses' face because of the glory of his countenance (2Cor 3.7). From then on, Moses would put a veil over his face whenever he talked with the children of Israel but removed the veil whenever he went up the mountain to meet with God. Apostle Paul described the glory on the face of Moses as a passing glory.

Referring to believers, Apostle Paul argues, 'If what is passing away was glorious, what remains is much more glorious.' (2Cor 3.11). Apart from Jesus Christ's transfiguration on the mountain, no human apart from Moses has been publicly known to be so transformed into the image of God. There may be unrecorded cases. However, it should be the hope of every believer that he/she can be transformed into the image and likeness of our Lord Jesus Christ, not when he/she is dead but while he/she is alive. (1Joh 1.2-3, 2Cor 3.12). 'But we all, with unveiled face, beholding as in a mirror the glory of the Lord, are being transformed into the same image from glory to glory, just as by the Spirit of the Lord.' (2 Cor 3.18). This is my hope. It is our hope.

Chapter 7

The Ten Commandments

The children of Israel knew about the gods of the Canaanites and the gods of the Egyptians before their experience at the foot of Mountain Sinai, so God first introduced Himself to identify which god they were going to have a covenant with to worship and serve. It was extremely important to identify the name and the type of god the children of Israel were dealing with because it would influence their lives and their destiny.

I am the Lord your God, who brought you out of the land of Egypt, out of the house of bondage.

(Exo 20.2)

Israel could recall how the Lord delivered them from the king of Egypt, the most powerful king on earth, and how He opened the Red Sea for them to walk through on dry ground when the army of Egypt pursued them. They could still see His presence above, protecting and guiding them. So, the children of Israel had no doubt who and which god they were dealing with. The Hebrew word for Lord is Jehovah or Yahweh and God is Elohim. 'I am Jehovah, your Elohim.' *Jehovah/Yahweh* is derived from the Hebrew word '*hayah,*' meaning self-existing and self-sufficient. According to Jewish tradition, the name *Jehovah/Yahweh* was too holy to be mentioned, so it was usually written without the vowels as YHWH (Tetragrammaton). The children of Israel instead used the word *Adonai* as a substitute for *Jehovah/Yahweh* (Gen 18.3).

Jehovah was a God of intimacy who sought and encouraged a closer relationship. It was Elohim who created the heavens and the earth but Jehovah Elohim who breathed into Adam to become a living being. It was Jehovah Elohim who put Adam in the garden in Eden and endowed him with glory, honour and dominion and visited him from time to time (Psa 8.4–8). It was Jehovah who proposed a covenant marriage with the children of Israel. When Jehovah revealed Himself to Moses, He said, 'I am Lord (Jehovah), I appeared to Abraham, to Isaac, and to Jacob as God Almighty (El Shaddai), but by My name Lord (Jehovah)! I was not known to them. I have also established My covenant with them, to give them the land of Canaan, the land of their pilgrimage, in which they were strangers.' (Ex 6.2–4).

God revealed the attributes of the name Jehovah in different ways to the children of Israel; Jehovah Nissi, Jehovah-Jireh, Jehovah-Rapha, etc. But the first distinct revelation of the name *Jehovah* was in connection with the redemption of the children of Israel. Therefore, Jehovah was a powerful redemptive name of God. Through the revelation of the name Jehovah, God began to unfold a personal relationship and communion with man, not only through His works but also through His manifest presence. Moses spoke to Him face to face or mouth to mouth. Through Jehovah's communion with the children of Israel, mankind began to know who God was, His nature and His character.

The first revelation of *Elohim* was in the creation of the heavens and the earth. 'In the beginning God (*Elohim*) created the heaven and the earth. The earth became a waste, void and chaos and darkness was over the earth.' Elohim was the name of the Creator God, who created the heavens and the earth and all that were in them. As we have already mentioned, *Elohim* is the plural form of '*El*,' but the Jews and the Christians translate it as a singular noun for the supreme God. Christians see the supreme God as a triune God, God the Father, God the Son, and God the Holy Spirit. In the Vine's Expository Dictionary and the Strong's Dictionary and Lexicon, the name *Elohim*, suggests strength, power, might, and pre-eminence. The Bible shows that *Elohim* has the attributes of omnipotence, omnipresence, and omniscience; all powerful, everywhere present and all knowing.

Prophet Jeremiah says, 'He (Elohim) has made the earth by His power; He has established the world by His wisdom, and has stretched out the heavens at His discretion.' (Jer 10.12). And King David declared, 'God (*Elohim)* has spoken once, twice I have heard this, that power belongs to God.' (Psa 62.11). Elohim was and is the God of miracles, signs, and wonders, as He demonstrated to Moses and all the children of Israel by bringing them out of Egypt and through the wilderness.

The backdrop of the Ten Commandments which God gave to the children of Israel was Baalism in the land of Canaan, so the Ten Commandments were antithesis to the practices of Baalism in Canaan. The Canaanites, as Baal worshippers, along with the Baal pantheon, indulged in abominable practices which defiled the land. As a result, they were dispossessed, and their land given to the children of Israel (Lev 18.24-25).

God warned the children of Israel, 'According to the doings of the land of Egypt, where you dwelt, you shall not do; and according to the doings of the land of Canaan, where I am bringing you, you shall not do; nor shall you walk in their ordinances. You shall observe My judgments and keep My ordinances, to walk in them: I am the Lord your God.' (Lev 18.3-4). 'You shall be holy, for I the Lord your God am holy.' (Lev 19.2). When Jehovah Elohim identified Himself from all the other gods, then He gave the Ten Commandments to the children of Israel. The first commandment was:

You shall have no other gods before Me.

(Exo 20.3, Deu 5.7)

The Hebrew word 'before' is *paniym*, meaning face, countenance, or presence, as we have seen above. 'You shall have no other

Elohim in my face or in my presence.' Jehovah Elohim was and is the Creator God, the Supreme, the Sovereign and the pre-eminent God. He declared through prophet Isaiah, 'Remember the former things of old, for I am God, and there is no other; I am God, and there is none like Me, declaring the end from the beginning, and from ancient times things that are not yet done, saying, 'My counsel shall stand, and I will do all My pleasure." (Isa 46.9-10). Jehovah God was and is distinct from all other gods and none could be compared with Him. The Psalmist asks, 'For who in the heavens can be compared to the Lord? Who among the sons of the mighty can be likened to the Lord? God is greatly to be feared in the assembly of the saints, and to be held in reverence by all those around Him.' (Psa 89.6-7).

To have another god before Jehovah God was and is to deny who He is. To deny who He is, is to kick Him out of His rightful position; to replace or displace Him. Apostle John says, 'Little children, keep yourselves from idols.' (1Joh 5.21). And Apostle Paul warns believers to flee from idolatry. 'Therefore, my beloved, flee from idolatry.' (1Cor 10.14). To flee implies to seek safety by flight or to escape safely out of danger. Idols could and can ruin one's relationship with God and destroy one's life.

The children of Israel were to be God's inheritance and His representatives on earth. All the other gods also had their own representatives or symbols on earth. If the children of Israel were to worship and serve any other god, they would of necessity serve, worship and be attached to their representatives or symbols on the earth; so Jehovah God gave the children of Israel the second commandment.

You shall not make for yourself a carved image – any likeness of anything that is in heaven above, or that is in the earth beneath, or that is in the water under the earth; you shall not bow down to them nor serve them. For I, the Lord your God, am a jealous God, visiting the iniquity of the fathers upon the children to the third and the fourth generations of those who hate Me, but showing mercy to thousands, to those who love Me and keep My commandments.

(Exo 20.4-6, Deu 5.8-10.)

Jehovah God told the children of Israel not to make carved images of any kind, worship them and serve them. The carved images were made by man as representatives or symbols of their gods. They were usually images of lower creatures like birds, animals, trees, fishes, etc. Those carved images would become the idols the children of Israel would worship and serve. Man is made far greater than any idol he can create. Apostle Paul says, 'Therefore, since we are the offspring of God, we ought not to think that the Divine nature is like gold or silver or stone, something shaped by art and man's devising.' (Act 17.29). So, he concludes that to worship and serve idols is foolish. 'Professing to be wise, they became fools and changed the glory of the incorruptible God into an image like corruptible man – and birds and four-footed animals and creeping things.' (Rom 1.22).

To bow down is to pay homage to a superior. The bowing, prostrating, kneeling, or kissing are the outward signs of inner submission or worship. In other words, the person places himself under the influence, dominion, and jurisdiction of that superior by performing the outward signs. The person then acquires the nature and the characteristics of the superior he/she bows to. Who you worship is who you become. The children of Israel created a golden calf and called it their god who brought them out of Egypt and began to worship it. Thereby the children of Israel began to take the nature and characteristics of Baal instead of Jehovah God; so they corrupted their hearts and corrupted themselves. To serve the gods would be to obey them and offer them their due, like sacrifices, offerings, praises, and festivals.

There is only one supreme and sovereign God in heaven, before whom everything and everyone in heaven worships and serves.

So, the right protocol which operates in heaven must also operate on earth. God said, 'I am the Lord, that is My name; and My glory I will not give to another, nor My praise to carved images.' Moses warned the children of Israel before they entered the Promised Land not to break the covenant because Jehovah was a jealous God. 'For the Lord your God is a consuming fire, a Jealous God.' (Deut 4.24). That is, the fire of His jealousy would burn and consume any corruption or unholiness before Him. An example was the consuming of Nadab and Abihu, sons of Aaron, before Jehovah. (Lev 10.1-2).

There are many Hebrew words that can be used for iniquity. But the one used here is 'avon'. It is derived from 'avah', meaning crookedness, perversion, guilt, misery, or iniquity. 'Avon' describes the offence, the punishment, and the guilt. It can serve as a collection of past offences against someone. Iniquity is normally connected with idolatry and is passed on from generation to generation. It is like a stubborn spiritual stain that pollutes and contaminates the gene pool and separates the family from God (Psa 51.2, Isa 59.2). Jehovah told the children of Israel that He would visit the iniquity of the parents to the third and the fourth generation. So the curse of iniquity would become a generational curse. But to those who loved Him He would show mercy to thousands; that is many generations.

The third commandment was:

You shall not take the name of the Lord your God in vain, for the Lord will not hold him guiltless who takes His name in vain.

(Exo 20.7, Deu 5.11)

The use of the phrase 'in vain' carries with it the sense of emptiness, falsehood, tastelessness, or nothingness. The name of Jehovah God portrays His pristine and incorruptible nature and His glory, and therefore the children of Israel were prohibited from using the name in anything that would stain, disrespect or profane who He was. The children of Israel could not even pronounce the name of Jehovah, but used a substitute name. Profaning the name might involve swearing, abuse, blasphemy, or gesturing. The name of Jehovah God was and is also higher and above any other name in heaven and on earth. It should not be misused in perjury like false swearing, empty oaths, and cursing. It should also not be used in any frivolous, meaningless, and vulgar language. The name of Jehovah was supposed to arouse awe and reverence among the children of Israel.

When the children of Israel moulded the golden calf and said, 'This is your god, O Israel, that brought you out of the land of Egypt,' they were using the name of Elohim in vain. They reduced the incorruptible and holy God to a golden calf made by human hands. That was blasphemy and disrespect. So, the children of Israel also broke the third commandment.

It is common to find God's name identified in things which are not of Him. And it is common to hear people swear, curse, and commit perjury using the name of God. It is not also uncommon to hear people use the name of Jesus Christ in frivolous, discourteous, disrespectful, needless, and vulgar manners, such as 'God Almighty,' 'Oh my God,' 'Jesus Christ,' or 'Jesus.' To many people it is just language, but to God it is not. Jehovah told the children of Israel that He would not hold anyone guiltless who used His name in vain. It was not only a command to the children of Israel but also to all humanity. James says, 'But above all, my brethren, do not swear, either by heaven or by earth or with any other oath. But let your 'Yes' be 'Yes,' and your 'No,' 'No,' lest you fall into judgment.' (Jas 5.12).

The fourth commandment was:

Remember the Sabbath day, to keep it holy. Six days you shall labour and do all your work, but the seventh day is the Sabbath of the Lord your God. In it you shall do no work: you, nor your son, nor your daughter, nor your male servant, nor your female servant, nor your cattle, nor your stranger who is within your gates. For in six days the Lord made the heavens and the earth, the sea, and all that is in them, and rested the seventh day. Therefore the Lord blessed the Sabbath day and hallowed it.

(Exo 20.8-11, Deu 5.12-15)

Jehovah later spoke to Moses and gave him further details of the Sabbath. 'Speak to the children of Israel, and say to them: The feasts of the Lord which you shall proclaim to be holy convocations, these are My feasts. Six days shall work be done, but the seventh day is a Sabbath of solemn rest, a holy convocation. You shall do no work on it; it is the Sabbath of the Lord in all your dwellings.' (Lev 23.2-3, Exo 16.23).

Sabbath is the first of the eight feasts which the Lord commanded. The word feast means an appointment, a fixed time or season, an appointed time or meeting. The feasts or festivals of the Lord were the appointed times and meetings with God. They were to be proclaimed as holy convocations. The Hebrew word for convocation is *miqua,* meaning something called out, public meeting, assembly, reading or rehearsal. The festivals were to be rest days or holy days (holidays) when public meetings were held to meet with the Lord and read and hear His word and worship Him. The children of Israel were not supposed to work but to keep the day in holy observance to the Lord God.

The eight festivals were Sabbath, Passover, Unleavened Bread, First fruits, Feast of weeks, Trumpets, Day of Atonement and Tabernacles. The children of Israel observed the Sabbath weekly on Saturdays to commemorate the day that Jehovah finished creating the heavens and the earth and rested. In the book of Deuteronomy, Moses included social and welfare reasons for observing the Sabbath day (Deu 5.15). The early church fathers, who were originally Jewish and had themselves celebrated Sabbath on Saturday, changed the Christian Sabbath to Sunday to commemorate the resurrection day of Jesus Christ (Acts 20.7, Luk 24.30-31, 1Cor 16.2). Sunday was the first day of creation and also the first day of the week. It was also the day Jesus Christ resurrected from the death and showed Himself to His disciples. It marked a complete change from the Old Covenant to the New Covenant in Christ Jesus.

The rest of the seven festivals were celebrated annually. The seven festivals painted and mapped out the prophetic picture of the redemption plan of God for mankind through Jesus Christ. When the children of Israel celebrated the feasts, they were also prophetically walking through the salvation plan of God through Jesus Christ. So, the festivals were rehearsals of the redemption plan of God. They were types which highlighted the earthly ministry of Jesus Christ in the Old Covenant. Jesus Christ fulfilled completely the spring feasts of Passover, Unleavened, First fruits, and Pentecost and will fulfil the winter feasts of the Trumpet, the feast of the Day of Atonement and the feast of Tabernacle in future.

When the church became the official religion under Emperor Constantine in 313 AD, he made certain changes to syncretise Christianity with the idol worship in the Roman Empire. Sunday was the official day of the sun god in the Roman Empire. In 321 AD, Constantine, with the support of the Roman Catholic Church, decreed that Christians should have their day of rest (Sabbath) on Sundays instead of Saturdays. So, some Christians sometimes see Sunday as a wrong Christian Sabbath or a pagan day. However, a careful look at the book of Acts will show that the apostles of Jesus Christ and the early disciples made that change themselves immediately after Jesus Christ was resurrected. They met on the first day of the week to break bread and to give their offerings (Acts 20.7, 1 Cor 16.2). Christians don't worship the sun god on Sundays as people say, but commemorate the resurrection day of Jesus Christ. It was and is the symbol of change from the Old

Covenant to the New Covenant. Others can also use Sundays to worship their gods.

Apostle Paul says, 'And let us consider one another in order to stir up love and good works, not forsaking the assembling of ourselves together, as is the manner of some, but exhorting one another, and so much the more as you see the Day approaching.' (Heb 10.24-25). Sabbath also pointed to a future millennium and eternal rest. Therefore, Sabbath has both literal and prophetic meaning and thus apply to Christians as well as the Jews.

The fifth commandment was:

Honour your father and your mother, that your days may be long upon the land which the Lord your God is giving you.

(Exo 20.12, Deu 5.16)

It is the first commandment that turned the attention of the children of Israel to their conduct or moral obligations. If they knew Jehovah and worshipped Him, then their conduct should reflect the nature of Jehovah. The Hebrew word for honour is *kabad*. It is a root word meaning to be heavy. In a good sense it could mean wealthy, honoured, esteemed, renowned, numerous, or glorious. In a bad sense it could mean dull, grievous, sinful, or severe. To honour your father and mother would have been to esteem them highly, to obey them, to celebrate them and to make them sufficient without any lack. It is the duty every child owes to his/her parents who have fed, nourished, cared, nurtured, supported, and defended them when the child was helpless, weak, and infant.

Honouring one's father and mother was commanded by God as a law. Why? Because the family is the foundational fabric of all human society, be it a family, a community, or a nation. It is the most important institution of human existence. The strength and the character of every nation boil down to the type of families who live in it. Therefore, the survival of every society or nation depends on the values of its families.

Secondly, the home is the best training ground for law and order, decency, integrity, respect for others and property. If the home is broken and divided and the child fails to learn these important lessons, it affects the child's social behaviour and his/her relationship with God. There is no doubt that what we frequently call 'juvenile delinquency' begins from broken and divided homes, undisciplined homes, or poorly managed homes.

Juvenile delinquency can lead to all sorts of behaviour patterns that can cost a lot of concern and financial loss to schools, neighbourhoods, communities, and the governments. Every government or generation must try and help keep the fabric of family life together. Anything that affects the family balance of a child will eventually lead to some future problems. Therefore, homes with same sex parents would be disadvantageous to children because they would need the import of both sexes to shape their future.

Thirdly, for every child, the parents become his/her first God. Parents represent God in the formative years of every child. Honouring God begins with honouring one's parents. It is therefore very important for every child to be taught to honour his/her father and mother. If a child does not learn to honour and esteem his/her parents who physically take care of him/her, it will be very difficult for him/her to honour and obey God. This commandment is sometimes placed with the first four commandment as one's commitment to God.

The fifth commandment says, 'that the days of the one who honours the father and mother might be long on the earth.' Apostle Paul advises children, 'Children, obey your parents in all things: for this is well pleasing unto the Lord.' (Col 3.20 KJV). 'Children, obey your parents in the Lord, for this is right. 'Honour your father and mother,' which is the first commandment with promise; that it may be well with you and you may live long on the earth. And you fathers, do not provoke your children to wrath, but bring them up in the training and admonition of the Lord.' (Eph 6.1-4).

It is the responsibility of the parents to train their children in godly and righteous living and in the fear of God. It is not the responsibility of teachers. Teachers follow their curriculum whether it is godly or ungodly. The Wisdom of Solomon says, 'The fear of the Lord is the beginning of wisdom, and the knowledge of the Holy One is understanding.' (Pro 9.10). The fear of the Lord also turns one away from evil and death and brings riches, honour, and long life (Pro 8.13, Pro14.27, Pro 22.4, Pro 10.27). So, the lack of proper home training and teaching of the word of God has a knock-on effect on our children, their families and the whole nation.

Commandments six to ten were:

You shall not murder. You shall not commit adultery. You shall not steal. You shall not bear false witness against your neighbour. You shall not covet your neighbour's house, wife, male servant, female servant, ox, donkey, nor anything that is your neighbour's.

(Exo 20.13-17, Deu 5.17-21)

The first four commandments put God at the top of the priorities and dealt with man's commitment to Him. The fifth commandment placed parents second on the ladder and dealt with man's commitment to them. The sixth to the tenth commandments put our neighbours third on the ladder and dealt with man's commitment to his neighbours. Those commandments dealt with how the children of Israel were to conduct themselves in a godly and moral manner among and in the midst of ungodly neighbours or nations. God first, family second, and neighbours third.

The children of Israel were going to live in a land in which the inhabitants imitated the evils of the gods they worshipped. The Canaanite gods, Baal and his pantheon, fought themselves, committed sexual immoralities, stole and coveted things for themselves and their subjects. The Canaanites copied the sexual immorality, fornication, adultery, incest, homosexuality, and bestiality of their gods. Jehovah warned the children of Israel not to do according to the doings of the Canaanites where He was bringing them (Lev 18.3).

The Hebrew word used for murder means to dash into pieces or to kill. It does not refer to the killing of enemies on the battlefield or to capital punishment, but to the deliberate killing of innocent lives. God caused the children of Israel to institute cities of refuge to shelter people who killed unintentionally. Regarding the ninth commandment, bearing false witness against a neighbour was a great injustice and sin that could lead to great loss, injustice, imprisonment or even death. It could result in character assassination and mar one's life for good. Bearing false witness can disrupt the fabric and the soul of every society. Does the society live by truth and function by right judgment or live by liars and function by false judgments?

The Ten Commandments were also the summary of the moral/judicial law, ceremonial/sacrificial law, and civil/religious law. The moral/judicial law dealt with the commandments spoken by a single living God, known to be Jehovah Elohim. It dealt with the character of God, His holiness, His righteousness, His love, and His goodness. The word spoken by Jehovah to Moses expressed and carried God's own image, likeness, and imprint. The ceremonial/sacrificial law dealt with laws concerning the ceremonies, festivals, and sacrificial practices. The civil/religious law dealt with the laws governing the daily lives of the children of Israel and their relationship with their neighbours. God later expanded or broke down the law into statutes, ordinances, and judgements.

We should not be in a hurry to throw away the Ten Commandments as Old Commandment stuff. As Jehovah God is the only Creator, Life-giver and Sustainer of the earth, His character, holiness, and righteousness should be reflected in every living being whom He has created in His image and according to His Likeness. So, the Ten Commandments apply to every individual irrespective of colour, creed, race, and religion. Each of the Ten Commandments is found in the New Testament in one form or another. Fragments of the Ten Commandments are found in many civil laws, decrees, and constitutions of societies and the nations of the world.

In the New Testament the Ten Commandments are summarised into two sections; the love of God and the love of the neighbour. 'You shall love the Lord your God with all your heart, with all your soul, with all your mind. This is the first and great commandment. And the second is like it. You shall love your neighbour as yourself. On these two commandments hang all the Law and the Prophets.' (Mat 22.37-39). The gospel of Mark says, 'There is no other commandment greater than these.' (Mar 12.31).

Jesus fulfilled the Law. He said, 'Do not think that I came to destroy the Law and the prophets. I did not come to destroy but to fulfil. For, assuredly, I say to you, till heaven and earth pass away, one jot or one tittle will by no means pass from the law till all is fulfilled.' (Mat 5.17-18). 'Jesus Christ is the end of the law for righteousness to everyone who believes,' and He is 'the author and the finisher of our faith.' 'In Him we should live, move and have our being.'

Jesus Christ was the last revelation of God on earth so that through faith the righteous requirement of the law might be fulfilled in us, not according to the flesh but according to the Spirit (Rom 8.3-4). We can only become the image and likeness of God through Jesus Christ by faith. So, no believer or New Testament saint can live outside of the Ten Commandments. To do that is to live in deception.

Chapter 8

The Golden Calf Generation

Moses came down from Mount Sinai on the fortieth day with the first set of the two tablets of stone on which God had written the Ten Commandments. The Ten Commandments, as I explained, represented God's image and likeness; His character and righteousness. Moses was to teach the children of Israel so that they would live in the shadow of God's image, likeness and righteousness and be transformed. The word Moses was bringing from God held the blueprint or the manual for the prosperity and the exaltation of the children of Israel (Exo 19.5-6, Deu 7.12-24, Deu 28.1-14).

But sadly, a day before Moses came down from Mount Sinai, on the thirty-ninth day, the children of Israel chose another god they wanted to worship, serve, and be transformed into. By moulding the golden calf, offering sacrifice, and proclaiming it their god, the children of Israel chose to use the wrong manual for their prosperity and exaltation. To use the wrong manual always carries serious consequences. The children of Israel, as descendants of Abraham, entitled to the blessings of Abraham's everlasting covenant with Jehovah, would be cut off from their blessings (Gen 17.7). God would no longer be their God and they would not be God's people. They would no longer be a kingdom of priests and a holy nation. In other words, they would lose their special favour as God's covenant people and be like any other nation.

When Moses came down the mountain and saw the moulded golden calf, the dancing, and the celebration of the children of Israel before the golden calf, his anger flared up and he cast the tablets out of his hands and broke them at the foot of the mountain. The tablets on which the Ten Commandments of God were written laid broken into pieces at the feet of the Baal-worshipping nation of Israel.

Apostle Paul reminds us that the pattern of events in the wilderness was an example to those who would live in the end times. 'Now all these things happened to them as examples, and they were written for our admonition, upon whom the ends of the ages have come.' (1Cor 10.11). This verse gives us a notice and a warning that the pattern of events which occurred in the wilderness journey of the children of Israel will repeat itself in the end times. People in the last days will turn once again to Baal or to idols for their journey of life.

Moses was a type of Jesus Christ, the only Redeemer and Mediator of mankind. Just before Jesus Christ returns to the earth there will be a golden calf generation, just like when Moses returned from the mountain and found a type of the golden calf generation at the foot of the mountain. The golden calf generation is the generation which would turn away from God and worship and serve idols (the Baal pantheon). It will be camped in a 'wilderness.' And the Ten Commandments or the righteousness of God (the word of God) would lie or be trampled under their feet. When this golden calf generation emerges, it will be a prophetic sign that the return of Jesus Christ is imminent and very close.

The children of Israel first dethroned Jehovah Elohim in their hearts. They wanted gods that would go before them. In other words, they wanted gods that would help them to reach their goal, the Promised Land, flowing with milk and honey. Moses had been with them through all the difficult times in Egypt, through the Red Sea and the harsh wilderness experiences. He had been called up the mountain by God and all that the children of Israel were thinking about was another way to fulfil their goal, with or without him. Moses did not seem important to them anymore. The overriding concern was to get to the

Promised Land and enjoy their prosperity. They assumed therefore that they would fare better with Baal than with Moses, the prophet of Jehovah. So, they broke their covenant with Jehovah out of their selfish desires.

Some of the reasons why people dethrone God in their hearts and turn away from Him are the lust for wealth, money, provision, power, position, fame, pleasure, sex, romance, success, comfort, etc. Like Eve, the devil deceived the children of Israel into thinking that they could be far better off without God. There is nothing wrong with the desire to have wealth, position, comfort, and the necessities of life legitimately. Nothing wrong with money or the fruit of a good legitimate business. The problem arises when we try to achieve our aim outside of God's righteousness and/or when the good desire turns into lust.

Lust is a strong desire or passion for what is forbidden or unlawful. Lust is selfish, deceptive, covetous, and controlling. It does not matter how many corners one cuts to be successful, how many poorer people one has to lie to or defraud to be successful, how many weak or common people one has to step upon or even destroy in order to be successful. Lust for wealth is always a deception because one has to trade off his/her soul in the end. Apostle Paul says, 'But those who desire to be rich fall into temptation and a snare, and into many foolish and harmful lusts which drown men in destruction and perdition. For the love of money is a root of all kinds of evil, for which some have strayed from the faith in their greediness and pieced themselves through with many sorrows.' (1Tim 6.9-10). Love of money in this passage means fond of money, greedy for money, avarice, or covetousness.

Jesus Christ asked this question: 'For what profit is it to a man if he gains the whole world, and loses his own soul? Or what will a man give in exchange for his soul?' (Mat 16.26, Mar 8.36). The gospel according to Luke puts it like this: 'For what profit is it to a man if he gains the whole world, and is himself destroyed or lost?' (Luk 9.25). Think about that. The end does not always justify the means.

For this you know, that no fornicator, unclean person, nor covetous man, who is an idolater, has any inheritance in the kingdom of Christ and God. Let no one deceive you with empty words, for because of these things the wrath of God comes upon the sons of disobedience, Therefore do not be partakers with them.

(Eph 5.5-7)

A covetous man, as is used in the passage above, is one eager for more, desiring for more or greedy for gain. The covetous person becomes an idolater when he/she bestows on his/her quest the affection or trust due to the true God. In other words, anything to which one offers undue affection and trust becomes an idol and dethrones God from His seat in the heart. The person has acquired another god and has becomes an idolater.

The passage also implies that an idol does not necessarily have to be a physical object or a physical image. An idol can be wealth, money, provision, power, position, fame, pleasure, sex, romance, success, comfort, self, property, someone etc. Some non-physical things or beings we give undue attention and affection to become our idols. In the heart the idolater still bows to the gods of wealth, money, power, position, fame, pleasure, sex, comfort, success, self, glamour, etc.

Who or what occupies the throne of one's heart determines one's idol. 'For where your treasure is, there your heart will be also.' (Mat 6.21). The Bible also says, 'as one thinks in his heart, so is he.' Man becomes the image of what is in his heart. He is corrupted by the corruption in his heart. So, when the children of Israel moulded the golden calf, sacrificed to it and worshipped it, they corrupted themselves. So is every man who has dethroned God in his heart and replaced Him with a corruptible object.

Apostle Paul, speaking about idolatry, said:

For since the creation of the world, His invisible attributes are clearly seen, being understood by the things that are made, even His eternal power and Godhead, so that they are without excuse. Professing to be wise, they became fools and changed the glory of the incorruptible God into an image made like corruptible men – and birds and four-footed animals and creeping things. Therefore God also gave them up to uncleanness, in the lusts of their hearts, to dishonour their bodies among themselves, who exchanged the truth of God for a lie, and worshipped and serve the creature rather than the Creator, who is blessed forever. Amen.

(Rom 1.20-25)

God's creation points to His nature and who He is. The Psalmist says, 'The heavens declare the glory of God; and the firmament shows His handiwork.' (Psa 19.1). It is possible to observe the wonders of creation and perceive the magnificence and the majesty of God. Instead of giving God the glory, man in his perverted earthly wisdom, chooses to give the glory of God to corruptible things which he has created himself.

Man, created in the image and likeness of God, is unlike any other creation. He is a representation of God on the earth. The only created being who has God's Spirit and the only being who can fully worship and testify to the glory of God. All other earthly beings are made lower than man and are intended to serve him. But man has forsaken God, given up his own position, turned away from the glory God intended for him and chosen to bow to other beings lower than himself.

God is Light and in Him is no darkness at all (1 Joh 1.5). He is the source of all wisdom, knowledge and understanding (Pro 8, Job 28). Whenever man forsakes God and walks away from Him, the light of God's wisdom, knowledge, and understanding becomes dim and man begins to walk in deception. God then gives him up or takes a step back from him and/or lifts His hand of protection and nurture from him. Thereafter, the deceptive glamour, the lawlessness, and the corruption which the world and the devil, the god of the world, bring into his heart can no longer be restrained. Man begins to heed and adopt these new voices or doctrines and adopt them into his life.

'Therefore God also gave them up to uncleanness, in the lusts of their hearts.' The word for uncleanness could also mean impurity and immorality in the heart, word, and deed. The heart is the centre of our thoughts, feelings, and concepts that frame our speech and actions. When therefore there are no righteous restraints to lust, then uncleanness, impurity or immorality begin to take over the mind and frame one's philosophy of life.

The purpose of this change of heart for idolaters is first to dishonour themselves or their bodies. In dishonouring themselves or their bodies, idolaters have to devalue, discredit, or demean themselves or their bodies. They have to change their mindset so that they can exchange truth for a lie and a lie for the truth. As the concept or the philosophy of their heart changes, then idolaters are able to serve and worship an idol or an image of lesser value, instead of serving and worshipping God, the Supreme Being. Without this change of heart, the demons behind the idols cannot influence the person.

The change in the heart may be motivated by one's family, culture, education, gene pool, DNA, religion, or experiences. It is almost impossible to overcome these ungodly influences and concepts altogether without God. These negative ungodly influences are not from God. They originate from man; many times they are passed on from the deeds of unknown past generations. When the person is hooked to these influences, even as a Christian, he/she becomes a captive, and he/she may not even know it. He/she can hear the truth in his/her ears but cannot hear it in his/her hearts. He/she can see the truth but cannot see it in his/her heart.

You may wonder why some people don't seem to understand what is naturally true, what is fair, what is noble and what is right. You may wonder why their belief system is so warped and utterly against what is naturally true, good, or honest. The heart! The heart controls our feelings and thoughts and thus our lives. The mind/brain accommodates and processes things that strengthen what we already believe in our hearts. God has given everyone a free-will. And He respects it. Man, or even a whole nation, chooses what it believes and frames its own future, whether good or bad, and takes responsibility for it.

From the 60s the world began to turn away from God and become more permissive. Since then, our desire to be free from God's moral standards has risen perceptively. We have become more insensitive to sin and more enculturated to unrighteousness. Our modern civilisation has redefined sin to suit its fleshy needs. The world, in our generation, is building its own Tower of Babel. Unholy pleasures which have no lasting value and benefit define many cultures today in our world. Using universal freedom or human rights as a cloak we have permitted inhuman and ungodly behaviours to flourish and dominate our world. There are whole generations of people who lead their lives away from God or outside of God. The church has become compliant to the present situation and therefore remains silent.

We desire to get away from God so that we can do what we want without any censure. This comes with a huge price tag. God lifts His hands from us, and we fall into the hands of another god, the god of this world, called Baal. In the Bible, the Jews called the devil Beelzebub (Baal zebub), the lord of flies or the lord of demons (Mat 12.24-27, Luk 11.15-18). The sad part is that the majority of people are not aware that when they fall or turn away from God, they fall into the hands of another god, Baal. They think they are free and can do what they want. But absolute freedom does not exist. If one is not accountable to God, then he/she is accountable to another superior being or thing.

Baal means lord. He was the chief Canaanite god, the god of fertility, god of life, god of the sky and heavens, god of the earth, god of rainfall, god of harvest, god of storm, thunder and fire, god of justice, protection and god of sex. Most of the non-physical idols people bow to today – wealth, money, power, position, fame, pleasure, sex, success, comfort, self, and leisure – were all embodied in the worship of Baal. Baal was and still is the god of mammon and materialism, the god that rules the world. Some people might not even have heard of the name of Baal, but when they worship these non-physical idols, they are worshipping Baal unknowingly.

So unconsciously, the world has gone back to worshipping the ancient Canaanite god of Baal in our modern civilisation. No doubt our civilisation is different from the Canaanites, and the mode of worship might be different, but the gods we worship and serve are the same gods the Canaanites worshipped and served. Apostle John cautions us:

Do not love the world or the things in the world. If anyone loves the world, the love of the Father is not in him. For all that is in the world – the lust of the flesh, the lust of the eyes and the pride of life – is not of the Father but is of the world. And the world is passing away, and the lust of it; but he who does the will of God abides for ever.' (1 Joh 2.15-17).

You see, the first Adam had everything; the power, the authority, and the kingdom. He was really the 'God' on earth, in-charge and in control of everything. But Eve, Adam's wife, was deceived to pursue her own selfish gain and roped her husband into it, so they lost all they had. The love of the world takes us away from God and we finally lose everything. Jesus categorically says, 'No one can serve two masters; for either he will hate the one and love the other, or else he will be loyal to the one and despise the other. You cannot serve God and mammon.' (Mat 6.24). Our world has evolved a materialistic culture, the Baal culture. And the same culture is deeply imbedded in our churches today.

Within the Christian fold there are nominal and intellectual Christians; those who say they are Christians but do not have any deep and heartfelt relationship with Jesus Christ. Jesus said, 'Not everyone who says to Me, 'Lord, Lord', shall enter the kingdom of heaven, but he who does the will of My Father in heaven.' (Mat 7.21). They have the gifts, alright, and have ministries, alright, but they work according to their own will. There are also those who truly have real, deep, and heartfelt relationships with Jesus Christ and do the will of God. This church divide has always been present, but in the end times the divide will widen and become more evident because there will no longer be a hiding place for one's true identity. You are either for Christ or you are not.

Apostle Paul wrote to the Thessalonians:

Let no one deceive you by any means; that Day will not come unless the falling away comes first, and the man of sin is revealed, the son of perdition who opposes and exalts himself above all that is called God or that is worshipped, so that he sits as God in the temple, showing himself that he is God.

(2 The 2.3-4)

'That day' refers to the return of our Lord Jesus Christ and the events surrounding it. So, Apostle Paul was saying that Jesus Christ will not return until there is a falling away. The Greek word for 'falling away' is *apostasia,* meaning defection from the truth or from the faith; apostasy. Many supposed Christians will renounce and/or abandon their faith in the gospel of Jesus Christ and denounce Christianity.

The apostasy that started gradually in the time of the early apostles will be more prominent and extensive in the end times. One of the main reasons why Christians will fall away from the faith is because they will find Baal worship or the temporal pleasures of this world more appealing and more enjoyable than the yoke of Christ.

The second thing which will happen before the coming of our Lord Jesus Christ is the revelation of the man of sin also called the son of perdition. These names are some of the names used by the Scripture to describe the antichrist. Antichrist comes from two words, *anti*, which means opposite, instead of, because of, and *Khristos*, which means anointed, referring to the Messiah, Jesus Christ; so the antichrist is one who opposes and denies Christ; against Christ and falsely presents himself as the Christ. There has been and is an antichrist system and culture since the dawn of Christianity (2 Joh 1.7). But there will be a person in the last days personified as the final antichrist (1Joh 2.18). This final antichrist must be revealed before the coming of Jesus Christ.

Apostle Paul warns again of people departing from the faith:

Now the Spirit expressly says that in the latter times some will depart from the faith, giving heed to deceiving spirits and doctrines of demons, speaking lies in hypocrisy, having their own conscience seared with hot iron, forbidding to marry, and commanding to abstain from foods which God created to be received with thanksgiving by those who believe and know the truth.

(1Tim 4.1-2)

The Greek word for depart is *aphistemi*. It comes from two words, *apo*, meaning 'from' or 'of' and *histemi* meaning stand. So *aphistemi* means to stand off or to stand from. In this case the people in the last days will stand away from the word of God while embracing and applauding doctrines of demons. From what we have learnt, they will applaud the doctrines of Baalism.

For the time will come when they will not endure sound doctrine, but according to their own desires, because they have itching ears, they will heap up for themselves teachers; and they will turn their ears away from the truth and be turned aside to fables.

But you be watchful in all things; endure afflictions, do the work
of an evangelist, fulfil your ministry.

(2 Tim 4.3–4)

Apostle Paul warned his spiritual son, Timothy, to be watchful
in the end times because people would no longer endure sound
doctrine. In other words, they would not endure uncorrupted
and wholesome doctrine. Christians today have been lolled into
the belief that all they have to do is to speak the word or pray to
God to shower wealth, prosperity, and blessings on them. They
have concentrated only on certain parts of the Bible and closed
their hearts to other parts of the Bible. They want to hear only
messages that promise more earthly benefits; wealth, prosperity, and enjoyment. Some of them move from place to place in
search of such messages. They are at every prophetic conference
and meeting that brings such messages, copying notes. 'They have
a form of godliness but deny its power.' (2 Tim 3.5).

Such Christians applaud these messages and the minsters who
bring them but turn away from what the Bible is really saying
to our time. They ran away from due spiritual process, correc-
tion or training, sacrifice, accountability, and judgment. They
really don't know the ways of the God they purport to serve and
for that reason they listen to deceivers, demonic voices, and false
prophets. Listening to such messages destroys one's belief system
and unknowingly defiles one's spiritual body and true identity
in Christ. I believe that the last days apostasy has already begun.

Billy Graham Evangelical Association UK published a survey in
2021 by the National Centre for Social Research (NCSR). In
the article it was revealed that 66% of the population in UK described themselves as Christians in 1983, 50% in 2008 and 38%
in 2018. They concluded that the UK is becoming more secularised because of young people being unaffiliated or identified
with any religion (None).

BBC News published Census 2001 in UK and showed that 71.75% of the population in England and Wales declared themselves as Christians, with the Muslims as the second largest religion with 2.97% and No Religion (None) with 14.81%. The same News media, BBC News, also published an article on the 2011 Census in UK. In this article, it showed that the number of people in England and Wales who identified themselves as Christians declined from 72% to 59% and a significant increase in the percentage of those who described themselves as having 'No religion' (None), from 15% to 25%. The writer said it was a sign of the religion's weakening influence in society. The census confirmed to me the rise of secularisation in UK. The Office for National Statistics (ONS) confirmed these figures with its publication in December 2012; a decline of 71.7% to 59.3% for Christians and an increase of the 'No Religion' (None) from 14.8% to 25.1%. It was widely predicted that the percentage of Christians in the 2021 census would drop below 50%.

Wikipedia, the free encyclopaedia, also confirmed the rise of secularisation in UK. It reported a Eurostat's Eurobarometer in December 2018, in which it was found that 53.6% of the UK's population were Christians, and 40.2% were non-religious (30.3% Agnostics, 9.9% Atheists). The May 2019 Special Eurobarometer found that 50% were Christians and 37% non-religious (9% atheists, 28% 'nonbelievers and agnostics').

In a separate publication in 2021, Wikipedia reported that atheism and agnosticism have increased among the general population in Europe, with falling church attendance and membership in many countries. The countries where most people reported no religious belief included France (40%), Czech Republic (37%), Sweden (34%), Netherlands (30%), Estonia (29%), Germany (27%), Belgium (27%) and Slovenia (26%). The countries with lesser no religious belief were Romania (1% non-believers) and Malta (2% non-believers).

The significant decline of religiosity and the rise of secularism is another way of saying that our society is rejecting the reality of God and moving away from Him. Apart from the atheists and the agnostics, the younger generation has chosen to be unaffiliated to any religious group. So, the trend of the rise of secularism will continue to increase over the coming years as the elderly leave the scene. All these facts indicate that Christianity has been declining at a rapid rate in UK and other places and will continue to do so.

The same trend is found not only in UK and Europe but also in many other countries. Statista, a German database company, published a survey in 2019 that 90% of American adults identified themselves as Christians in 1970, the figure dropped to 80% in 2000 and in the late 2010s it dropped further to 71%. Gallup, a global management consulting company, published an article that membership in houses of worship (Churches, synagogues, and mosques) in the USA continued to decline and had fallen below 50% for the first time in 2020. Membership had previously been about 70% in the last decade and dropped to 50% in 2018 and 47% in 2020.

The decline in church membership in the USA was said to be primarily a function of the increasing number of Americans who expressed 'no religion' preference. The percentage of Americans who did not identify with any religion grew from 8% in 1998-2000 to 13% in 2008-2010 and 21% in 2018-2020. A drop of about 20% membership in houses of worship and a rise of about 13% non-affiliates (None) is very significant. The same decline in religiosity is happening in most of the advanced countries, like Canada and France. Win-Gallup International in a 2012 poll found that 48% of Australians claimed no religion and 37% declared themselves as Christians. Christianity still remains the largest religious body in the world, about 30%, Islam about 25%, and the third is 'No religion' (None), about 15%. It is my humble submission that the percentage of 'No religion affiliates' will overtake that of the religious affiliates in future.

I have already made mention that if one turns away from God, he/ she falls into the hands of another god, in this case Baal. Idolatry today, as it has always been, affects our social, economic, and political lives. Idolatry, undoubtedly, is the trending culture of our day. Our modern civilisation seems to think that the word of God is ancient, unfashionable, and outdated. We have developed our own righteousness to please our fleshy nature. The world seems to think that deep-seated Godly beliefs are signs of weakness, inferiority, or bigotry. In some nations Godly beliefs are repressed and state worship is encouraged. However, if one looks closely at our modern-day culture, one will find similar patterns in the Bible of people who moved away from God and fell into the hands of other gods, to their own detriment. The world had already begun to walk on the road that led to the flood judgment in the days of Noah and the fire judgment in the days of Lot.

At the foot of Mount Sinai, the children of Israel turned away from God. They proclaimed a new festival and offered burnt offerings and peace offerings to Baal. I have already mentioned that whenever people change their god, they must also of necessity change their festivals and celebrations. The type of festivals and celebrations always point to the type of gods the people worship and serve.

In our civilisation, we celebrate many festivals, some global, some national, some religious, some regional and some local. Do they represent certain gods? Many do! We may not realise that by our participation in these festivities we are worshipping certain gods. One of the global festivals we celebrate is Christmas. Christmas is a festival which we celebrate on the 25th of December, every year, as the birth of Jesus Christ. However, it has very little or nothing to do with Jesus Christ or His birth. First, the Bible does not specify a date for the birth of Jesus Christ nor give any instruction for its celebration. Even a cursory review of the birth of Jesus Christ in the Bible shows that He could not have been born on the 25th December, in the middle of winter.

However, there were other pagan deities who were known to have been born to virgins on the 25th December. Notable of these deities were Horus, the Egyptian god of the sky and war; Attis, the Phrygian god of vegetation; Mithras, the Roman god of the sun and light; Krishna, the Hindu god of compassion, tenderness and love and Dionysus, the Greek god of fertility, wine and pleasure. 25th December was therefore the Roman Empire's official birthday of Mithras, the sun god (Sol Invictus). When the Roman Catholic Church became the official religion of the Roman Empire, it adopted 25th December as the official birthday of Jesus Christ in 336 AD. 25th December was also dated among several pre-Christian pagan festivals connected with the winter solstice. Other things which have now become part of the Christmas celebration, like the Christmas tree, Santa Claus, holly, ivy, or giving of presents, all have pagan roots. So, at Christmas, we definitely don't celebrate the birth of Jesus Christ. The question is what do we celebrate, and which deities do we worship at Christmas?

The death of Jesus Christ as the last Passover Lamb sealed the celebration of the Passover for Christians. Christians should not celebrate the Jewish Passover but should commemorate the death and the resurrection of our Lord Jesus Christ. The Holy Communion celebrated as often as possible is the only festive meal Jesus Christ instituted for Christians. However, some of the pre-Christian pagan festivities connected with spring equinox have crept into the Christian Easter celebration. The bunnies, the Easter eggs, Easter buns, Easter cakes etc. were all connected to pagan festivities in the past. True Easter celebration of the death and the resurrection of Jesus Christ has been hijacked by commercialised pagan festivities. Christians should not allow themselves to be sucked into these commercialised pagan festivities of Easter. Christmas, Easter, and many other festivals we celebrate give indications of the types of gods nations and the world worship, and they are backed by big multi-billion-dollar businesses.

The children of Israel, at the foot of Mount Sinai 'sat down to eat and drink.' In other words, they had a feast or a party after sacrificing to their new god. Apostle Paul writes, 'And do not become idolaters as were some of them. 'The people sat down to eat and drink, and rose up to play.'' (1 Cor 10.7). Apostle Paul was warning the Corinthians not to partake food and drink in festivals and parties organised in honour of idols, similar to the episode of the golden calf in the wilderness. The children of Israel sought to cover their tracks by saying that it was the feast to the Lord. But it wasn't. It was a feast to Baal. In other words, what name you give to a party does not matter; what matters is whom the party really honours. What is the partying about? Which god or image does the party honour?

The way the children of Israel 'sat down to eat and drink' also made them to be labelled as idolaters. It gives the impression that they took the food and drink in excess. They lusted after the food and drink. That was part of the attraction of Baal worship, to do what the worshippers wanted to do without censure or care. The food and drink were consumed in abundance to satisfy the lusts and appetites of their baser human nature.

They also 'rose up to play.' I have already mentioned that the Hebrew word for 'play' means to laugh, mock, play, dance, make a sport of or make a toy of; it was the same word used by Potiphar's wife to indicate that Joseph had tried to sexually assault her (Gen 39.14). Therefore it suggests some sort of licentious, unlawful sexual activities. The wild and loud parties of food and drinks many times push people over the edge to commit abominable sins which they regret later. It was all part of the worship of Baal.

As our society becomes more secularised and permissive, so does the increase of sexual immorality. Our opinion of sex has changed over the years. We are increasingly taking sex for granted and treating it as a normal way of enjoyment and entertainment. So, there are sexual suggestions everywhere you turn. It seems to dominate our world, on television, social media, music, magazines, book etc. Perhaps because of modern advances, teen pregnancy has reduced over the years, according to recent statistics. Baal is usually not worshipped alone but worshipped with Asherah, the mother goddess, or the goddess Ashtoreth.

'They forsook the Lord and served Baal and Ashtoreths.' (Jud 2.13, Jud 10.6, 1 Sam 7.4). Ashtoreth was the Sidonian goddess of lust, lovemaking, beauty, desire, sensuality, and military pomp (1Kin 11.5, 1Kin 11.33, 2Kin 23.13). She was the twin sister of the goddess Anath. Sidon was the firstborn of Canaan (Gen 10.15) and therefore inherited a lot of the Canaanite corruption. Goddess Ashtoreth was the Jewish equivalent of the Greek goddess Aphrodite and the Roman goddess Venus. She was sometimes seen as the consort of Baal and sometimes as the consort of Molech. She was known to be connected to child sacrifice and homosexuality.

The goddess Ashtoreth (Aphrodite and Venus) was normally symbolised by beautiful young nude woman with exposed breasts. She was supposed to have the power to seduce both the gods and men into sexual practices. Therefore, to dress provocatively to expose one's intimate body parts, like one's breast, back, or thigh is a type of worship to goddess Ashtoreth.

In our present civilisation, sexually explicit exposures are warmly accepted and applauded. Many people, especially woman dress to expose their intimate body parts to gain acceptance or popularity. Products sell better and women have more fans when they expose more of their intimate body parts. One would find this exposure of intimate body parts on television, on social media, in bars, restaurants, hotels, motels and private meetings as part of our enjoyment and entertainment. Our present civilisation has turned to the worship of the ancient goddess Ashtoreth (Aphrodite and Venus). We applaud and celebrate those who worship these goddesses as superstars and role models.

Many Christian women have copied the worldly fashion and go to church meetings in the same attitude, exposing their intimate body parts. They think that since everyone accepts the trending worldly fashion, God also accepts it. However, their dresses and demeanours mark them as subjects of goddess Ashtoreth (Aphrodite or Venus). They have turned their churches into temples of the goddess Ashtoreth. While their dresses are signifying that they are worshippers of the goddess Ashtoreth, they are praising the Lord Jesus Christ and even ascribing their behaviour to Him. Delusion! Those who are privileged to stand before others to sing or preach, if they are not careful, will release the spirit of these goddesses into the atmosphere and grieve the Holy Spirit. The obvious question is whom do they really worship and serve? Ashtoreth, Aphrodite, Venus, or Jehovah God?

Joshua, at the end of his life, asked the children of Israel to choose whom they wanted to serve. He concluded, 'But as for me and my house we will serve the Lord.' (Jos 24.15). The children of Israel insisted that they would serve the Lord. So Joshua charged them, 'Now therefore ... put away the foreign gods which are among you, and incline your heart to the Lord God of Israel.' (Jos 24.23). These Christian women who have copied the world fashion into their churches, must choose whom they really want to worship and serve. 'No one can serve two masters... You cannot serve God and mammon.' (Mat 6.24). They cannot serve Ashtoreth and Jehovah God as the same time. If they choose to worship and serve Jehovah God and His Son, Jesus Christ, then they should put away the regalia of goddess Ashtoreth (Aphrodite or Venus). Let your conducts be in line with your hearts.

Apostle Paul points out that when one become an idolater, whether with a physical or non-physical image, he/she first exchanges the truth of God for a lie, dishonours his/her body in order to worship and serve an idol. The next stepdown is to become a sexual deviant.

For this reason, God gave them up to vile passions, for even their women exchanged the natural use for what is against nature. Likewise, the men, leaving the natural use of the woman, burned in their lust for one another, men with men committing what is shameful, and receiving in themselves the penalty of their error which was due (Rom 1.26-27).

The Greek word for vile is *atimia*. The same word is translated as dishonour in verse 24, which we have said also means to devalue, discredit, or demean. If idolatry continues without repentance, God further removes His hand of care and nurture so that the lust of the heart gives way to dishonourable passion and affection. The Greek word for passion, *pathos,* comes from *petho,* to wound, hurt, or suffer. Lexical Aids to the New Testament describes *pathos* as a soul's diseased condition, out of which various lusts spring. Idolatry therefore corrupts the soul. The first sign of this diseased condition is to dishonour themselves or their bodies to worship and serve an idol, then follows vile passions or affections.

These vile passions or affections are manifested outwardly by the women exchanging the natural use for what is against nature; that is practising lesbianism. And the men leaving the natural use of the women, lust after men; that is practising homosexuality. It would seem that homosexuality has its roots in some form of idolatry. In the ancient worship of Baal, homosexual and sodomic practices formed part of its normal way of worship. So, homosexuality or sodomy connects the practitioners to Baal worship. Whether they know it or not and whether they like it or not makes no difference.

Apostle Paul labelled homosexuality or sodomy as an error. Its Greek meaning is wandering, one led astray from the right way, deceit, delusion, or error. These wanderers or deluded people, according to Apostle Paul, 'receive in themselves the penalty of their error which was due' (Rom 1.27). The word 'penalty' means a reward or a recompense and the word 'due' means that which is necessary, needed, ought, right and proper. First, according to Apostle Paul there are penalties for the error of homosexuality or sodomy, and secondly, the penalties are right and proper. Apostle Paul did not specify the type of penalties, but whatever it is, it may negatively affect the spiritual and physical well-being of the person.

From what we have said so far, it can be argued that God did not create homosexual orientations as people are saying today. It would be very unfair for God to create one as a lesbian or a homosexual and turn round to condemn the same person. There can be many reasons why a person becomes a lesbian or a homosexual, but God is not the author of them. God condemned those practices strongly in Leviticus chapter eighteen. Apostle Paul was saying that somewhere, somehow there was a link of lesbianism, homosexuality, and sodomy to idolatry. You see, the true fact is that if any society turns away from the true God and worships idols (physical or non-physical), these unnatural orientations and identities increase among its people. The good news is that Jesus Christ defeated the devil on the cross (Col 2.15). Therefore, these unnatural sexual behaviours can be broken in the name of Jesus Christ and man can be set free.

Apostle Paul advised the church to flee sexual immorality. 'Flee fornication. Every sin that a man doeth is without the body but he that committeth fornication sinneth against his own body.' (1 Cor 6.18, KJV). Fornication here means illicit sexual intercourse and it includes adultery, lesbianism, homosexuality, and bestiality. That was and is a direct command to run away from fornication. Paul says that every sin that a man commits is outside the body, but the sin of fornication is directly against the body. Apostle Paul had earlier explained, 'Or do you not know that he who is joined to a harlot is one body with her?' For the two, He says, 'shall become one flesh.' (1 Cor 6.16). In fornication one becomes one flesh with another body outside the covenant of

God. Fornication therefore defiles and corrupts the body and is likely to affect one's gene pool.

Such an unauthorised union and bond with another body dishonours and corrupts the presence of the Holy Spirit, who inhabits the body. 'Or do you not know that your body is the temple of the Holy Spirit who is in you, whom you have from God, and you are not your own? For you were bought as a price; therefore glorify God in your body and in your spirit, which are God's.' (1Cor 6.19-20). Fornication strikes directly against the relationship between a believer and the Holy Spirit. Fornication is also a spiritual union of two souls. Therefore, it works against both the physical body and the spiritual body. Because in sexual intercourse the two become one, fornication is also a major doorway for the transference of unsolicited diseases and unclean spirits from one person to another.

Homosexuality among men is usually called sodomy. Sodomy is anal sexual intercourse. The principle behind sodomy is seed mismanagement. The live sperms of man are not put in the right place but in the wrong place. So the semen, which contains the sperm, is flushed out as waste. The whole practice is meant for temporary pleasure with no consideration for fruitfulness or the future. The basic building block of any nation is the family unit. These homosexual practices therefore run against the basic fabric of any family, society, or nation. The end result of homosexuality or sodomy is sterility and fruitlessness, as exemplified by what happened to Sodom and the cities around it.

The whole land is brimstone, salt, and burning; it is not sown, nor does it bear, not does any grass grow there, like the overthrow of Sodom and Gomorrah, Adamah and Zeboiim, which the Lord overthrew in His anger and wrath.

(Deut 29.23)

God rained brimstone and fire on the land of Sodom and Gomorrah to such an extent that the land lost its fruitfulness and could not maintain vegetation again. Such was the end result of homosexuality or sodomy in Sodom and the cities around it. Apostle Peter explained that the punishment of Sodom and Gomorrah was an example to those who afterward would live ungodly, and Jude likened it to the final judgment of eternal fire. (2 Pet 2.6, Jud 1.7). Could the fruitlessness and the sterility be the recompense Apostle Paul was talking about?

The Bible says that sexual immorality defiles the practitioners and also defiles the land itself so that the land vomits out both the practitioners and the non-practitioners (Lev 18.25). Therefore, fornication affects everyone living on the land. The Bible calls Lot righteous but he was oppressed by the filthy conduct of the people. Lot was a wealthy man, but he lost all his riches, his business, his home, and his wife in Sodom. (2Pet 2.7, Gen19.23-26). Where do we live today, in Egypt, in the wilderness, or in Sodom?

God sent the children of Israel to Canaan, the land of promise, 'flowing with milk and honey.' The chief god of the Canaanites who occupied the land of promise was Baal. Baal, among other titles, was the male god of fertility. One of Baal's consorts was his own mother Asherah, mother goddess, the goddess of fertility and love. Another of Baal's consort was his sister, Anath, the goddess of love and war. The Canaanites and later the children of Israel thought that the fruitfulness and the abundant harvest of the land of promise were due to the sexual intercourse between Baal and his consorts. So, all forms of fornication were practised freely as part of the worship of Baal and Asherah. People who engage in fornication may not realise that they are indirectly worshipping the Canaanite god of Baal and the goddess Asherah (or Ashtoreth).

I am speaking not from any special holiness on my part, nor any special knowledge and wisdom, but from the patterns God has laid out for mankind in the Bible. The patterns in the Bible give us previews of what will happen in the future. Whether we believe it or not, whether we like it or not, they are repeated in future generations. God 'declares the end from the beginning' (Isa 46.9-10). If we sincerely take an impartial look at the history of mankind, we will discover that the patterns in the Bible have been repeated in one form or the other in different and future generations. And it will continue to do so right to the end of time.

What I think about sexual immorality does not matter. What matters is what God thinks. According to God's word, my main concern is four-fold. One, so far as the Bible or God's word is concerned, all forms of sexual immorality are sinful. Two, according to word of God, all forms of immoral sexual practices bring defilement to the practitioners and desolation to the land where they are practised. Three, countless number of innocent people who are not practitioners are also affected. Four, the rise of homosexuality gives a prophetic pointer to the last days.

Our culture has changed. Homosexuality, which had been on the fringes of our society has in the last 50 years become part of our cultural norms. People are now openly gay and openly lesbian. There are now more homosexual bars, homosexual clubs, homosexual entertainments, homosexual music, and others at almost every corner of the world. Same-sex marriage is legalised and accepted all over the world, especially in the more advanced countries. Baal worshippers of old hated the sanctity of marriage between a man and a woman and the sanctity of a stable home. These things are indications that our culture has evolved and broken down the religious bedrock on which our society once stood into a more non-religious culture. We have begun walking on the similar road which provoked God's anger to destroy Sodom and Gomorrah. If we follow the pattern in the Bible, the end result will also be desolation and destruction.

In Wikipedia's demographics of sexual orientation, it is reported that in Australia, 4.1% men and 2.8% women identified as homosexual in 2014. In Canada, 5.3% identified as LGBT in 2012. In France, 3% identified as bisexual and 4% as homosexual in 2014. In Germany, a female-only survey found 5% German women identified as gay or bisexual in 2017. In Japan, data estimated that 8.9%, aged 20-59 years were LGBT in 2018. In Mexico, 6% were identified as homosexual and 5% as bisexual in 2017. In Spain, 6% were male homosexuals, 3% female homosexuals and 2% bisexuals in 2017. In the United Kingdom, 3.5% identified as gay and 2.4 as bisexual in 2017. In the USA 4.5% identified as LGBT in 2017. LGBT means lesbian, gay, bisexual, and transgender (more letters have been added but I prefer to stick with the basic).

According to the same Wikipedia, German LGBT were identified as 6.9% in 2019 and according to the Foundation Jasmin Roy Survey (LGBT Realities), 13% of the Canadian population belonged to LGBT. According to Gallup, a global management consulting company, LGBT identification rose to 5.6% in USA in 2020. If a global overview of the population of LGBT is carried out in the last ten years, it would be found that there is a significant increase in the LGBT population all over the world. The significant increase in the population of LGBT is an indication that our society is shifting gradually but surely towards a LGBT culture and same sex-marriage culture.

Allied to sexual immorality of the Canaanites was the practice of incest. In our world today, the practice of incest is legal in some nations and states and illegal in others. The nature of the relationship included in the laws of incest also differs from one area to another. There is no doubt that the practice of incest is prevalent. In the United Kingdom, the Crime Survey for England and Wales (CSEW) estimated in 2019 that 7.5% of adults aged 18 to 74 years experienced sexual abuse before the age of 16. The National Society for the Prevention of Cruelty to Children Learning (NSPCC, Learning), reported of a study with young people which estimated that 1 in 20 children in the UK have been sexually abused. The abusers were mostly people they already knew. Considering the fact that many of the cases of sexual abuse remain unreported in order to protect family and loved ones, we can say that incest and child sexual abuse are prevalent.

In the USA, Rape, Abuse & Incest National Network (RAINN) estimates that 1 in 9 girls and 1 in 53 boys under the age of eighteen experience sexual abuse or attack at the hands of an adult. It is known that the effects of sexual abuse are long-lasting and affect the victims' mental health. The problem of incest and child sexual abuse cuts across most tribes, communities, and nations. The advent of internet culture has also highlighted online child sexual exploitation. Some of the perpetrators are apprehended but others are not.

Before the Lord Jesus Christ returns these sexual sins will be common and escalate in our world. LGBT will increase in power. Religious groups should be aware of this. There is nothing they can do about it. As our culture evolves and accommodates these changes, some religious bodies, like Christianity, Judaism and Islam will come under severe form of persecution from these groups and the public. This persecution will be empowered by the rise of goddess Ashtoreth and the spirit of Jezebel (Dan 7.21, Rev 17.6). What is happening in our world today in connection with sexual sins is not by accident. It should tell us that the return of the Lord Jesus Christ is not far off at all.

At the foot of Mount Sinai, before the children of Israel, laid the broken pieces of the tablets of the Ten Commandments on which was inscribed the sixth commandment. 'You shall not murder.' I have already explained that it does not refer to the killing of enemies on the battlefield or to capital punishment but to the deliberate taking of innocent lives. The worshippers of Baal sacrificed their own sons and daughters hoping to gain great favours or benefits. They deprived their unborn children their God-given lives and that of their generations unborn because of their own selfish pursuits. God told Noah and his household after the flood, 'Whoever sheds man's blood, by man his blood shall be shed; for in the image of God He made man.' (Gen 9.6). Man is made in the image and likeness of God, so nobody has the right to take another person's life.

The shedding of innocent blood defiles the land and drives God away from the land. 'So you shall not pollute the land where you are; for the blood defiles the land, and no atonement can be made for the land for the blood that is shed on it, except by the blood of him who shed it. Therefore do not defile the land which you inhabit in the midst of which I dwell; for the Lord dwell among the children of Israel.' (Num 35.33, Lev 20.2-3). God told Cain when he killed his brother, Abel, 'When you till the ground, it shall no longer yield its strength to you...' (Gen 4.12). The shedding of innocent lives robs the land of its fruitfulness.

Do not defile yourselves with any of these things; for by all these the nations are defiled, which I am casting out before you. For the land is defiled; therefore I visit the punishment of its iniquity upon it, and the land vomits out its inhabitants.

(Lev 18.24)

'These things' referred to the sexual immoralities and the child sacrifices of the Canaanites. The bloodshed which defiled the land would also defile the people, the sanctuary of God and His holy name. God told the children of Israel not to allow their children to pass through the fires of Molech (Lev 18.21, Deu 18.10).

God cautioned the children of Israel not to pollute the land with bloodshed, otherwise the land would vomit them out as it did to the nations before them (Lev 18.28). Child sacrifice was punishable by death, and if anyone turned blind eyes or became indifferent to child sacrifice then God would set His face against him, his family and cut him off (Lev 20.1-5). Therefore, every member of the community shared in the curses of child sacrifice. It was and is a serious offence.

Child sacrifice started early in human history with the worship of idols and has continued since that time. Today the greatest bulk of child sacrifice or shedding of innocent blood is through abortion. Abortion is simply the termination of a pregnancy in order to stop the birth of a child. Millions of innocent babies are aborted all over the world each year for non-medical reasons.

It is not difficult to see the divide and emotions that accompany this issue. There are the pro-choice groups which advocate for a woman's basic right to choose whether to have children and when to have them. In other words, women have the right to choose between unplanned pregnancy and abortion. Denying a woman the right to abortion is denying her fundamental rights. Pro-choice groups, also referred to as abortion rights movements, support legalisation of abortion. There are also the pro-abortion groups which support the view that women should have the right to have abortion if they choose to do so.

At the other end are the pro-life or anti-abortion groups which advocate that all human lives are created equal regardless of size, level of development, education, and level of dependency. Therefore, intentionally terminating the life of pre-born baby is a violation of the fundamental rights of life. Pro-life groups therefore do not support abortion or the legalisation of abortion and euthanasia.

The issues that sharply divide the pro-abortionist and the anti-abortionist include ethical, moral, religious, scientific, medical, political, and other considerations. So, the issue of abortion can be complex or diverse and many times rake up a lot of emotion and passion. What I think about abortion is not the issue. It is what God thinks about abortion. That's my main concern here. We can understand what our scientists, medical experts and our psychologists say about abortion, but in the end, it is the Creator's voice and His righteousness alone that will judge mankind.

God told Jeremiah that He knew him before he formed him in his mother's womb. 'Before I formed you in the womb I knew you; before you were born I sanctified you; I ordained you a prophet to the nations' (Jer 1.5). There are other interpretations, but my simple understanding is that Jeremiah was formed and existed before his birth. If he was spiritually alive before birth, then he was alive in the womb of his mother the first day of the pregnancy. The moment the 23 chromosomes of his father and the 23 chromosomes of his mother were paired to form the 46 chromosomes of the foetus, Jeremiah's full total make-up was unalterably determined. All it needed was for the foetus to be processed in time. I believe it is so with every man.

Jeremiah later remarked, 'Because He did not kill me from the womb that my mother might have been my grave, and her womb always enlarged with me. Why did I come forth from the womb to see labour and sorrow, that my days should be consumed with shame?' (Jer 20.17). This clearly shows that Jeremiah was alive in the womb of his mother.

Apostle John referring to Jesus Christ as the true Light says, 'In Him was life, and the life was the light of men... That was the true Light which gives light to every man coming into the world.' If every man receives life before coming into the world, then he/she must be alive in the mother's womb the first day of his conception. So, to wilfully terminate a foetus would be an act of murder in the eyes of God.

There is a key consideration in this abortion divide: 'When does life begin?' Various groups have differing answers to this question; at conception, at implantation, when the fertilised egg is implanted in the womb, embryonic stage, from the third week, at the first movement of the foetus, about 16 to 17 weeks after fertilisation, at tissue separation, at the first sign of brain activity, at the viability of the foetus, when it can survive outside the womb at birth. So there seems to be no agreement as to the definite time when life begins in the womb.

Abortion is not expressly mentioned in the whole Bible. It is true, there is really no specific law in favour of abortion or against abortion in the Bible. However, as we have seen in the case of Jeremiah, the Bible is clear about the fact that an unborn child is precious in the eyes of God. David said:

For You formed my inwards parts; you covered me in my mother's womb. I will praise you, for I am fearfully and wonderfully made; marvellous are Your works, and that my soul knows very well. My frame was not hidden from You, when I was made in secret, and skilfully wrought in the lowest parts of the earth. Your eyes saw my substance, being yet unformed. And in Your book they all were written, the days fashioned for me, when as yet there were none on them.

(Psa 139.13-16)

The eyes of God saw the foetus of David and even when he was unborn, his destiny was determined and written in God's book. The angel Gabriel told Zachariah about his son, John the Baptist, 'For he will be great in the sight of the Lord, and shall drink neither wine nor strong drink. He will also be filled with the Holy Spirit, even from his mother's womb... he will also go before Him in the spirit and power of Elijah, to turn the hearts of the fathers to the children, and the disobedient to the wisdom of the just, to make ready a people prepared for the Lord.' (Luk 1.15-17).

Jesus Christ, referring to John the Baptist, also said, 'And if you are willing to receive it, he is Elijah who is to come. He who has ears to hear, let him!' (Mat 11-14-15). Elijah was translated long before the birth of John the Baptist. If John the Baptist was the Elijah to come and was to be filled with the Holy Spirit from his mother's womb, then he might have been alive in his mother's womb from day one. We can also mention Jesus Christ Himself, God the Word, who became flesh. He was alive from day one in the womb of Mary, His mother (Luk 1.35). Imagine Mary decided to abort her pregnancy because of the tradition and the norms of her day.

So, even though the Bible does not mention abortion specifically, it is clear that the Bible favours the view that life begins at conception. Of course, there are other professionals and groups, even religious groups, who have other reasons to disagree. I don't argue with them, I speak purely from the viewpoint of the Holy Bible. If we accept the view that life does not begin at conception, then we need to find out when life begins? However, if we accept the view that life begins at conception, then it is murder to intentionally abort a child at any stage of the pregnancy.

God said to Cain when he murdered his brother, Abel, 'What have you done? The voice of your brother's blood cries out to Me from the ground. So you are cursed from the earth, which has opened its mouth to receive you brother's blood from your hand.' (Gen 4.10-11). Now, think about the millions of abortions each year and imagine the cries of these innocent unborn babies crying to God for vengeance.

I sincerely believe that when a nation legalises abortion, that nation has cursed itself and has signed a legal deed with the devil for more bloodshed. That nation has released spirits of murder and death upon the land. Do we wonder why innocent blood is been shed more and more in some countries? Nobody is safe, even in the security of his/her own home or in public, in schools, colleges, bars, churches and on our streets. Nations which decriminalise abortion have pronounced God's judgement upon themselves whether they believe it or not. The voices of the blood of these innocently murdered children also begins to cry to God, calling for vengeance, and the cycle continues. There is always the cry of bloodshed in the atmosphere. 'These six things the Lord hates, yes, seven are an abomination to Him: a proud look, a lying tongue, hands that shed innocent blood, a heart that devises wicked plans, feet that are swift in running to evil, a false witness who speaks lies, and one who sows discord among brethren.' (Pro 6.16-19).

According to the World Health Organisation (WHO), there are about 40 million to 50 million abortions in the world every year. According to the World Population Review, China has an abortion rate of 24 per 1,000 women. With China's population of about 1.3 billion, China carries out about 31 million abortions every year. The USA has an abortion rate of 20 per every 1,000 women. With the population of about 328 million, the USA carries out about 6.5 million abortions every year. Russia has the highest abortion rate of 53.7 per 1,000 women. With the population of 144 million, Russia carries out about 7.7 million abortions every year.

One of the major sins in the land of Canaan, including Sodom and Gomorrah and the cities around them, in the days of Lot was the sacrifice of children to Baal and Molech. However, the number of abortions, child sacrifices, carried out by our civilisation is many times greater than that of the Canaanites in the days of Lot. As God judged the Canaanites and the children of Israel who later committed child sacrifices, so God will also judge any civilisation which practises child sacrifice. This pattern is already set for us in the Bible. The level of the shedding of innocent lives should give us an indication that we are much closer to the second coming of our Lord Jesus Christ than we think.

Some of us think that we can safely hide under the argument that abortion is not a sin against God. What about if it is? Can we risk it? Let's look around with open minds, we shall find that God's righteous indignation is already at work in some nations which have legalised abortion. Everyone in such a nation pays a price for abortion whether he/she participates in it or not.

When one becomes an idolater, the third descending fall, according to Apostle Paul, is a debased mind.

And even as they did not like to retain God in their knowledge, God gave them over to a debase mind, to do those things which are not fitting; being filled with all unrighteousness, sexual immorality, wickedness, covetousness, maliciousness, full of envy, murder, strife, deceit, evil-mindedness; they are whisperers, backbiters, haters of God, violent, proud, boasters, inventors of evil things, disobedient to parents, undiscerning, untrustworthy, unloving, unforgiving, unmerciful; who knowing the righteous judgement of God that those who practice such things are deserving of death, not only do the same but also approve of those who practise them.

Rom 1.28-32

In the first descending fall, God gave up the idolaters to uncleanness in the lusts of their hearts. In the second fall, God gave them up to vile affections. In the third fall, God gave them up to a debased mind. The Greek word use for debased, *adokimos*, means unapproved, rejected, worthless and reprobate. A person with a debased mind has his intellect, understanding and emotions filled with worthless and reprobate things. It all begins from one source, idolatry. One will argue that all these characteristics mentioned by Paul have been part of human existence since the world began. That's true, because idolatry started very early in human existence. But as we get closer to the return of Jesus Christ, these characteristics will be more prominent and predominant as confirmed by Paul's letter to Timothy.

But know this, that in the last days perilous times will come: For men will be lovers of themselves, lovers of money, boasters, proud, blasphemers, disobedient to parents, unthankful, unholy, unloving, unforgiving, slanderers, without self-control, brutal, despisers of good, traitors, headstrong, haughty, lovers of pleasure rather than lovers of God, having a form of godliness but denying its power. And from such people turn away! For of this sort are those who creep into households and make captives of gullible women loaded down with sins, led away by various lusts, always learning and never able to come to the knowledge of the truth. Now as Jannes and Jambres resisted Moses, so do these also resist the truth, men of corrupt minds, disapproved concerning the faith; but they will progress no further, for their folly will be manifest to all, as theirs also was.

(2 Tim 3.1-9)

The message of Paul to Timothy revealed how these malicious and unloving characteristics would be more prevalent in the last days. It would reveal how far we have moved away from the holy, loving, merciful and compassionate God. It all starts with falling away from God and embracing idols (whether physical or non-physical). The powers or demons behind the idols are relentless, marching their captives to desolation and eternal destruction.

As God has said, 'I will dwell in them and walk among them, I will be their God, and they shall be My people. Therefore 'Come out from among them and be separate, says the Lord. Do not touch what is unclean and I will be a Father to you, and you shall be My sons and daughters, says the Lord Almighty.' (2 Cor 6.16-18). People of God cannot share in the sins and/or the pleasures of idolatry and expect to be free of judgment just because they are born again or pray in tongues. 'Stop drinking the wine of abominations and fornication.' Don't be a partaker of the corruption of this world.

This is a prophetic call. Come out!

Chapter 9

Back To God

If we turn again to the golden calf episode, God told Moses on the mountain top that his people had corrupted themselves. They had made a moulded calf, worshipped it, sacrificed to it, and called it their god. Yet when Moses came down from the top of Mount Sinai to the camp of the children of Israel, his anger became so hot that he threw the tablets of the Ten Commandments in his hands and broke them at the foot of the mountain.

Moses first identified the golden calf and the source of the loud singing and the exuberant dancing. He then took the responsibility upon himself and destroyed the golden calf. What he did was contrary to the new culture, the popular opinion in the camp. Moses knew that so far as the idol remained, the people were still in bondage and could not be delivered from its influence. To turn back to God, that idol (the golden calf) and its altar must be destroyed.

When the children of Israel entered the promised land, in the days of the judges, they forsook the Lord God and served the gods of the Amorites. God's anger was provoked, and He delivered them into the hands of the Midianites for seven years. The Midianites and their Amalekite accomplices would come and destroy the produce and vegetation of the children of Israel and leave no sustenance for them. The children of Israel were therefore greatly impoverished and cried to the Lord God. The Lord God sent them a judge, a deliverer, called Gideon.

The first task God gave Gideon was to destroy the source of the idolatry. 'Take your father's young bull, the second bull of seven years old, and tear down the altar of Baal that you father has, and cut down the wooden image besides it; and build an altar to the Lord your God on top of this rock in the proper arrangement, and take the second bull and offer a burnt sacrifice with the wood of the image which you shall cut down.' (Jud 6.25-26).

The wooden image represented Asherah, the goddess of fertility and love and the consort of Baal. Jehovah God told Gideon the source of the idolatry which had pervaded and corrupted the nation of Israel. Gideon had to accomplish that first task before he could deliver the children of Israel from the Midianites and the Amalekites.

Gideon was born into Baal worship. His father might have been the priest or the caretaker of Baal. The whole family worshipped and served Baal. The whole community and the whole nation also worshipped and served Baal. Baalism was part of their normal way of life and culture. To tear down the altar of Baal and to cut down the wooden image of Asherah was a very tough assignment. One that will tear apart his own family and expose him to scorn, hatred, attack, and even death. 'But because he feared his father's household and the men of the city, he did it by night.' (Jud 6.27b). Surely, the men of the city tried to kill him, but failed.

It is not surprising that in today's society if anybody tries to touch abortion or homosexuality, the person comes under fierce unwarranted hatred, abuse, and attacks. This hatred, abuse and these attacks would come from the same people who preach democracy and freedom of speech. This is a simple indication that our society and culture want to remain in Baalism. They try to frighten people, threaten them, and forced them to remain silent or capitulate. But the fact is that if we want to turn back to God, then the idols of Baal, Asherah and Ashtoreth must be torn down at all costs. If not, even though we call ourselves Christians or believers, we will still be captives and subjects of these gods and not enter the kingdom of God (1Cor 6.9-11, Eph 5.5-7).

As I explained in the last chapter, an idol is anything that has replaced God in one's heart. So, one must first identify who and what occupies the throne of his/her heart. Is it your own self, your wife/husband, your children, your job, lust for money, fame, power, sex, success, comfort etc.? To be frank, although the idols may be glaring to others, it may not be easy to identify by yourself. One does not easily admit and take responsibility for any wrongdoing until he/she is found out. Looking at ourselves, we can easily justify all our decisions and actions. It will be painful and difficult to acknowledge any wrongdoing or any character flaw by oneself, so one may have to seek help from those around him/her and also employ the help of the Holy Spirit. The Holy Spirit is the Spirit of truth, who will not lie to you. If one is sincerely serious about needing the help of the Holy Spirit, he/she will receive help.

Once the idol or idols occupying the throne of one's heart are found, then begins the battle to dethrone and destroy them. Moses identified and destroyed the golden calf of the children of Israel. Gideon also tore down the altar of Baal and Asherah of his family and the people. The children of Israel were instructed how to deal with the Canaanite idols. 'But thus you shall deal with them; you shall destroy their altars, and breaks down their sacred pillars, and cut down their wooden images and burn their carved images with fire.' (Deu 7.5). Abraham was completely removed from his idolatrous background to the Promised Land. Jesus Christ said:

If anyone desires to come after Me, let him deny himself, and take up his cross daily and follow Me. For whoever desires to save his life will lose it, but whoever loses his life for my sake will save it.

(Luk 9.23-24)

The cross is an instrument of death. In other words, one can only follow Christ as a living death. The Greek word here for life is

159

psuche. It means breath or soul. If anybody wants to protect, keep, and retain his/her soul life, he/she will eventually lose it. Soul life includes activities of the soul, such as desires, feelings, emotions, thoughts, imaginations, choices, reasoning and will. The soul which is corrupted by these activities will be destroyed. But he/she who brings his/her soul life to death will save it. That is, he/she who denies his/her soul life for the sake of Christ will save the soul because it will not be destroyed by the fire of judgement. However, if one blows the opportunity to put his/her soul life to death on the earth, he/she would lose it altogether in heaven. 'There will be weeping and gnashing of teeth.'

In the camp of the children of Israel, when Moses saw that the people were unrestrained, he stood at the entrance of the camp and said, 'Whoever is on the Lord's side – come to me!' And all the sons of Levi gathered themselves to him (Exo 32.26). So, the time came for the people in the camp of Israel to make a stand either for Baal or for God. The choice one makes either to stick with Baal or turn back to God will require some costly sacrifices.

The cost of sticking with Baal will be losing your heavenly inheritance eternally, as we have said above. The cost of turning back to God may cause you to break family ties, old ties, friendships, and acquaintances. One may come under reproach, scorn, abuse, persecution, and even death for you and your loved ones. One may lose his/her job, business, contract, his/her fame, position, office, power, and wealth. It may be very costly to turn back to God in a golden calf generation, but the end will be worth it. Can you pay the price?

Many Christians believe that Jesus Christ paid it all on the cross so there is no need for any further sacrifice. I beg to disagree. Apostle Peter, who loved Jesus Christ, walked with Him physically and saw Him crucified on the cross, later wrote:

For to this you were called, because Christ also suffered for us, leaving us an example, that you should follow His steps.

1 Pet 2.21

The Greek word example is *hupogrammos*, meaning an underwriting or a written copy to be copied or imitated, an example. We are expected to suffer for His sake. We, the church, are the body of Christ on earth. Therefore, there is some amount of suffering the church, you and I, have to go through to complete the work of Christ on earth. Apostle Paul says, 'The Spirit Himself bears witness with our spirit that we are children of God, and if children, then heirs – heirs of God and joint heirs with Christ, if indeed we suffer with Him, that we may also be glorified together.' (Rom 8.16-17). In other words, one cannot be glorified with Him if one does not suffer with Him. He said, 'I now rejoice in my suffering for you, and fill up in my flesh what is lacking in the afflictions of Christ, for the sake of His body, which is the church.' (Col 1.24).

Apostle Peter says this about the trials of a believer: 'In this you greatly rejoice, though now for a little while, if need be, you have been grieved by various trials, that the genuineness of your faith, being much more precious than gold, that perishes, though it is tested by fire, and be found to praise, honour, and glory at the revelation of Jesus Christ.' (1 Pet 1.6-7). James says, 'My brethren, count it all joy when you fall into various trials, knowing that the testing of your faith produces patience. But let patience have its perfect work, that you may be perfect and complete, lacking nothing.' (Jam 1.2-4). So, the manifold trials of life are seen by Peter and James as the test of faith.

Apostle Peter was crucified upside down and James was beheaded for the sake of the gospel of Jesus Christ. Martyrdom has been part of the church's journey since its inauguration at the Jerusalem Pentecost, two thousand years ago. Apart from Apostle John, all the apostles of Jesus Christ were martyred in the nations of the world. Many others have died since and many continue to die for Christ's sake. Each of them will receive a martyr's crown. At the end of his life, Apostle Paul said, 'I have fought the good fight, I have finished the race, I have kept the faith. Finally, there is laid up for me the crown of righteousness, which the Lord, the righteous Judge, will give to me on that Day, and not to me only but also to all who have loved His appearing.' (2Tim 4-7-8). He also remarked, 'For I consider that the suffering of this present time are not worthy to be compared with the glory which shall be revealed in us.' (Rom 8.18).

When the golden calf and its altar in the camp of the children of Israel were destroyed, then Moses went back to the top of Mount Sinai to seek atonement for the sins of Israel. 'You have committed a great sin. So now I will go up to the Lord, perhaps I can make atonement for your sin.' (Exo 32.30). The Hebrew word for atonement is *kaphar*, meaning to cover or pardon. So, sin has to be covered before God in order not to incur His wrath. Since the wages of sin is death, God has decreed that innocent blood should be used to cover sin.

For the life of the flesh is in the blood, and I have given it to you upon the altar to make atonement for your souls; for it is the blood that makes atonement for the soul.

(Lev 17.11)

'According to the Law almost all things are purified with blood, and without shedding of blood there is no remission.' In our turning back to God, there must be a period of repentance. Repentance is not just being sorry for the sin, but a genuine change of the heart and mindset. Moses did not go up the mountain and could not have gone up the mountain with any animal blood. But on the mountain Moses became the substitute in supplication and offered himself for the sin of the children of Israel, thereby becoming a foreshadowing of Jesus Christ. 'Not with the blood of goats and calves but with His own blood He (Jesus Christ) entered the Most Holy Place once for all, having obtained eternal redemption.' (Heb 9.12).

The intercession of Moses for the sin of the children of Israel was able to avert God's judgement for about 700 years. When we put our own lives on the line for the sake of Jesus Christ on behalf of others, it gains us great favour before God, just like Jesus Christ. Apostle Peter confirms that the heavens and the earth will certainly come under judgement (2Pet 3.7). Judgement will definitely come, but when it comes, the world might be judged because it followed the pattern of the Old Testament and didn't repent.

If My people who are called by My name will humble themselves, and pray and seek My face, and turn from their wicked ways, then I will hear from heaven, and will forgive their sin and heal their land.

2 Chr 7.14

If the nations of the world humble themselves, repent and call on the name of God, and turn from their sins, God will forgive the world and heal the land. I wish it is that simple. To the church in Thyatira Jesus talked about Jezebel: 'I gave her time to repent of her sexual immorality, and she did not repent. Indeed I will cast her into a sickbed, and those who commit adultery with her into great tribulation, unless they repent of their deeds.' (Rev 2.21-22). God has given the world enough time.

The question is whether the world is ready to repent. In our individual private prayers and church prayers, repentance might be going on. But is the whole world ready to repent? Even if we limit repentance to the church, are the churches of the world ready to put aside their denominational differences, tribal differences, doctrinal differences, and episcopal differences and come together to truly pray and seek the face of the Lord? I doubt it. The coming judgment, however, is not even going to be on the church alone but on the whole world.

In Prophet Joel's days, God called the people to repentance in connection to the plague of the land. 'Now, therefore, says the Lord, 'Turn to me with all your heart, with fasting, with weeping, and with mourning.' Prophet Joel took up the call to repentance.

So rend your heart, and not your garments; return to the Lord your God, for He is gracious and merciful, slow to anger, and of great kindness; and He relents from doing harm. Who knows if He will turn and relent, and leave a blessing behind Him – a grain offering and a drink offering for the Lord your God? Blow the trumpet in Zion, consecrate a fast, call a sacred assembly; gather the people, sanctify the congregation, assemble the elders, gather the children and nursing babes; let the bridegroom go out from his chamber, and the bride from her dressing room. Let the priests, who minister to the lord, weep between the porch and the altar; let them say, "Spare Your people, O Lord, and do not give Your heritage to reproach, that the nations should rule over them. What should they say among the peoples, 'Where is their God?'

(Joe 2.13-17)

Prophet Joel seemed to suggest that the outer court prayers will not work. Many people might be praying, but it is only cosmetic and superficial prayers. Their purpose, perhaps, is to give one the impression that they are also praying, but there is no real conviction. They may rend their garments as a show of their grief, but not their hearts. Rending of the garments and/or outward show of grief and sorrow alone will not move God. The prayers that will move the hand of God are those that cut deep into the heart and tear the heart into pieces.

The Wisdom of Solomon writes, 'keep your heart with diligence, for out of it spring the issues of life.' (Prov 4.23). The heart here refers to the centre of man's being. The very core of one's being must grief for sin and turn from Baal to God. Prophet Joel did not exempt anybody, the elders, the children, the nursing babes; even the bridegroom, the bride and the priests were called to fasting and sanctification. Can we do the same thing? Will our leaders, the politicians, the elite, and the celebrities bow before God publicly and lead the people to repentance? I doubt it. What about the rich, the wealthy and the famous? I doubt it.

In the prophetic judgement of Prophet Ezekiel, the Lord called those 'men' who had charge over the city of Judah. Six 'men' came up, each with his battle-axe and one man clothed with linen with a writer's inkhorn at his side. God instructed the 'man' with the writer's inkhorn at his side thus. 'Go through the midst of the city, through the midst of Jerusalem, and put a mark on the forehead of the men who sigh and cry over all the abomination that are done within it.' (Ezek 9.4).

They were the men who sighed, groaned, mourned, lamented, and cried over the abominations of Judah. Their cry and mourning might have been in private and not in public. But the important thing was that inwardly they were lamenting for the ungodliness in the land and longing for the righteousness and holiness of God to be revealed.

God told the other six men who had charge over the Judah, 'Go after him through the city and kill; do not let your eye spare, nor have any pity. Utterly slay old and young men, maidens and little children and women; but do not come near anyone on whom is the mark; and begin at the sanctuary.' (Ezek 9.5-6). God's anger was poured not only on the perpetrators but also on those who supported them, those who were complacent and sympathetic with those sins, including those who kept silent about them.

If one looks intently at the wrath of God against the land and the people in the Scripture, our repentance should include three areas of sins that affect the land. They are the sin of idolatry, the sin of sexual immorality, and the sin of shedding innocent blood. The land in which we live has been polluted and corrupted by these sins over hundreds of years and is ready to vomit us out. Some of the problems we face are due to the fact that the land or creation is corrupted, polluted by our sins. Our land needs cleansing and healing to give support to righteous people and righteous living. The cleansing and healing will come only by the grace and mercy of God through repentance.

Before the glory of the Lord left the temple, God took Ezekiel to see every sort of creeping thing, abominable beasts and all the idols of Israel portrayed on the walls in the temple and worshipped by seventy elders of the house of Israel (Eze 8.10-12). He took Ezekiel into the inner court of the temple to see twenty-five men facing east and worshipping the sun (Eze 8.16-17). Who says idolatry is not in the church? It is right in the centre of many churches.

God will shake the church until there is a remnant or His bride has made herself ready. 'Yet once more I shake not only the earth, but also the heaven.' Now this 'Yet once more' indicates the removal of those things that are being shaken, as of things that are made, that the things which cannot be shaken may remain. Therefore, since we are receiving a kingdom which cannot be shaken, let us have grace, by which we may serve God acceptably with reverence and godly fear. For God is a consuming fire. (Heb 12.26-29).

The church will be the first to be shaken because judgement will begin with her (1 Pet 4.17). The shaking might take many forms, like persecution and oppression from individual, earthly governments, and nations. Something will happen that will separate the half-baked Christians and the fleshy Christians from the remnant. Looking at the carnal church of today, the demonic cultic system and the antichrist systems in the world, the apostasy, and the rebellion to the gospel of the kingdom, the judgement of God will affect every area of our lives.

We all need the grace to pray and pray aright. The Holy Spirit will help us in our weakness if we are really serious to get out of the Baal system. 'Likewise the Spirit also helps in our weaknesses. For we do not know what we should pray for as we ought, but the Spirit Himself makes intercession for us with groanings which cannot be uttered.' (Rom 8.26).

And I will pour on the house of David and on the inhabitants of Jerusalem the Spirit of grace and supplication; then they will look on Me whom they pieced. Yes they will mourn for Him as one mourns for his only son and grieve for Him as one grieves for a firstborn.

(Zec 12.10)

This Scripture obviously refers first to the Jews. They would come to know Jesus Christ as the true Messiah, and they will enter into a sincere and deep mourning and repentance for the past and reach out for Him. The Scripture could also refer to all those who have rejected the Lordship of Christ. As it affects the house of David, the Scripture can also refer to the church which is reaching out for revival in the end times. God will pour upon them the Spirit of grace and the Spirit of Supplication.

The Hebrew word for grace is 'chen'. It means favour, kindness, grace, loveliness, charm, and preciousness. The outpouring of the Holy Spirit will bring these blessings upon the church. The Hebrew word for supplication is tachanun. It means earnest prayer, entreaty, or supplication. The word formerly portrayed a picture of an olive-branch waved by the supplicant, seeking peace, mercy, and surrender. It was not a private prayer or merely a prayer of meditation but a vocal or public demonstration of surrender.

When the Spirit of Supplication is poured over the world, there will be cries for mercy and for help all over the world. There will be weeping, mourning, brokenness, surrender and true repentance. 'Lord, I surrender – I can't fight you anymore, I can't reject you any longer. I have fought against you but now I give up.' 'I am a sinner and I am lost. There is no hope for me. Please forgive me, have mercy on me and take me back. I am weak, worn, torn, wounded and tired. Please save me. I surrender my spirit my soul and my body to you.' Then the seed of the gospel will germinate very quickly in their hearts.

When the Spirit of supplication is poured on the church, it will weep and grieve over sin, the lost and the dying world. The church will begin to pray for and live in holiness, godliness, and purity. Titus says, 'Teaching us that, denying ungodliness and worldly lust, we should live soberly, righteously and godly in the present age.' (Tit 2.11-13). People will begin to pursue peace and holiness, without which no one will see God. One of the prayer points of today's church is to pour upon her the spirit of grace and supplication. This is not praying against the devil, as we usually do in intercession, but reaching out to God.

God finally told Moses to make new tablets to replace those he broke at the foot of the mountain, and he would write on them the same commandments He wrote on the first set of tablets. (Exo 34.1-4). We have already concluded that the two set of tablets were symbols of human hearts. After repentance, one needs a new heart. Sometimes the heart is equated to the spirit of man. 'The spirit of man is the lamp of the Lord, searching all the inner depths of his heart.' (Pro 20.27).

The spirit of man is the interface, the place God meets with man. It is God's altar. Jesus says, 'But if the eye is bad, your whole body will be full of darkness. If therefore the light that is in you is darkness, how great is that darkness!' (Mat 6.23). Sometimes the altar, the spirit or the heart is broken down, and ruined.

There is no longer any light in it. The heart, the spirit, needs to be repaired and rebuilt first, as Elijah did on Mount Carmel (1 Kin 18.30). Then the fire of God came upon the altar through Elijah's prayers. We also need the fire of God upon the altars of our hearts again by prayers, fasting and waiting on the Lord. The fire of God will destroy all the corruption, pollution, and the uncleanness in our lives.

The best sacrifice on this newly prepared altar, is oneself. 'I beseech you therefore, brethren, by the mercies of God, that you present your bodies a living sacrifice, holy, acceptable to God, which is your reasonable service. And do not be conformed to this world, but be transformed by the renewing of your mind, that you may prove what is that good and acceptable and perfect will of God.' (Rom 12.1-2). Apostle Paul tells us the modus operandi.

Yet indeed I also count all things loss for the excellence of the knowledge of Christ Jesus my Lord, for whom I have suffered the loss of all things, and count them as rubbish, that I may gain Christ, and be found in Him, not having my own righteousness, which is from the law but that which is through faith in Christ, the righteousness which is from God, by faith; that I may know Him and the power of His resurrection and the fellowship of His suffering, being conformed to His death.

Phil 3.8-10

Apostle Paul had everything to gain by insisting on his Jewish heritage, his education, his standing in society and his religiosity. But he considered all of them as nothing and rubbish to gain Christ. Jesus Christ confirms the actions of Apostle Paul. 'So likewise, whoever of you does not forsake all that he has cannot be My disciple.'

A young ruler went to Jesus and asked Him a very important question. 'Good Teacher, what shall I do that I may inherit eternal life?' Jesus replied, 'Why do you call Me good? No one is good but One, that is, God. You know the commandments: 'Do not commit adultery,' 'Do not murder,' 'Do not steal,' 'Do not bear false witness,' 'Do not defraud,' 'Honour your father and your mother.'' And the young ruler said, 'Teacher, all these things I have kept from my youth.' Then Jesus looking at him, loved him and said to him, 'One thing you lack: Go on your way, sell whatever you have and give it to the poor, and you will have treasure in heaven; and come take up the cross, and follow Me.' But he was sad at this word, and went away sorrowful, for he had great possessions. Jesus later threw light on this. 'How hard it is for those who have riches to enter the kingdom of God!'

(Mar 10.17-23).

Scripture says Jesus' disciples were astonished at His words. But Jesus continued. 'Children, how hard it is for those who trust in riches to enter the kingdom of God! It is easier for a camel to go through the eye of a needle than for a rich man to enter the kingdom of God.' (Mar 10.24-25). It is obvious from what we have said that the rich man has replaced God with his/her riches in the heart and therefore has become an idolater. The riches have become his/her god. Idolaters cannot enter the kingdom of God. (1Cor 6.9-10, Eph 5.5).

Is it possible for a rich man to enter the kingdom of God? Yes, it is. Jesus said, 'With men it is impossible, but not with God; for with God all things are possible.' (Mar 10.27). For the rich to enter the kingdom of God, he must enthrone Jesus in his/her heart as Lord. In other words, his/her riches must come under the Lordship of Christ and therefore can be used whenever and wherever the Lord pleases. He/she will have to take himself/herself out of his/her riches. This is sticking point, to give out all I have worked hard for to the poor? Not to do whatever I want with my own riches?

On the top of Mount Sinai, God proceeded to make a new covenant with the children of Israel by writing His commandments on the second set of tablets. 'Behold the days are coming, says the Lord, when I will make a new covenant with the house of Israel and with the house of Judah … For this is the covenant that I will make with the house of Israel after those days, says the Lord: I will put My laws in their mind and write them on their hearts; and I will be their God and they shall be My people.' (Heb 8.10). So will God make a new covenant with you if you prepare your heart, keep it holy, undefiled from the world and do His will.

God promised that Elijah would come back before the coming of the Lord Jesus Christ.

Behold, I will send you Elijah the prophet before the coming of the great and dreadful day of the Lord. And he will turn the hearts of the fathers to their children and the hearts of the children to their fathers, lest I come and strike the earth with a curse.

(Mal 4.5-6)

Prophet Elijah confronted Jezebel and the Baalism in the days of King Ahab. The spirit of Elijah came back in the person of John the Baptist to herald the ministry and the person of Jesus Christ. He was the last Old Testament prophet. The head of John the Baptist head was cut off before the new covenant of Jesus Christ was established. Elijah will return to confront the end-time Jezebels and the proliferation of Baalism in the last days. In today's golden calf generation, when the proponents of Baalism are officially supported and dine with the mighty, people in power and authority, the famous and celebrities, it will require people with the spirit of Elijah to confront them.

Elijah challenged the prophets of Baal to a contest. They were to be given two bulls, one for the prophets of Baal and the other for Elijah. Each was to prepare the bull and put no fire on the altar. The prophets of Baal should call on the name of Baal and Elijah should call on the name of Jehovah God. And the God 'who answers by fire, He is God.'

Now we understand the bull was the symbol of Baal. And Baal was supposed to be the god of storm, thunderbolt, and fire. So, if Baal was a true God, then in all probability the prophets of Baal should have won the contest. But they cried all they could, shouted all they could, and even cut themselves until blood gushed out of them, but still there was no fire.

Then Elijah repaired the broken altar at Mount Carmel and put his sacrifice on the altar. He instructed that water should be poured on the sacrifice and the wood. They did it a third time so that the water ran all around the altar and filled the trench. Then he began to pray.

Lord God of Abraham, Isaac and Israel, let it be known this day that You are God in Israel and I am Your servant, and that I have done all these things at Your word. Hear me, O lord, hear me, that this people may know that You are the Lord God, and that You have turned their hearts back to you again.

(1 Kin 18.36-37)

'Then the fire of the Lord fell and consumed the burnt sacrifice, and the wood and the stones and the dust, and it licked up the water that was in the trench.' The fire of the Lord consumed not only the sacrifice, as one would expect in the tabernacle of Moses and in the temple, but everything, the altar, the wood, the stones and even the dust.

Now when all the people saw it, they fell on their faces; and they said, 'The Lord, He is God! The Lord, He is God!'

(1 Kin 18.39)

What happened was an eye-witness proof that Baal was not a living God, Jehovah was the living God. So, the people paid homage and reverence to the Lord God. The prophets of Baal were executed and the drought of Israel ended, but the revival of Elijah was short-lived. King Ahab and wife Jezebel continued with their idolatry, and so did the kings after them. The Jezebels and the Ahabs of the last days will come with greater power. So will the spirit of Elijah. Elijah left his mantle for his son, Elisha. But Elisha, who had the double spirit of his father, Elijah, died with his mantle. It was not left for anybody. I believe that it had to be so because the mantle of Elisha belongs to the end time saints.

Baalism must be defeated once again and for the last time. John the Baptist, who came in the spirit of Elijah, was not afraid to lose his head for the sake of the gospel. He was a herald to Jesus Christ. And the heralds of the second coming of our Lord Jesus Christ, in this golden calf generation, must possess the fearless spirit of John the Baptist and the double spirit of Elijah (Elisha) in order to overcome and defeat the Baalism and the Jezebels of the end times and usher in our Lord Jesus Christ.

Perhaps you are one of them.
God bless you.

The author

Solomon S. Aggrey is a Bible Teacher and Preacher
originally from Cape Coast, Ghana. He was first
ordained into the Anglican Communion in Nigeria
and became the Founder of the Temple of Shalom
Christian Church in Manchester, United Kingdom.
He has two adult children and enjoys reading and
writing. This is his second published work.

The publisher

*He who stops
getting better
stops being good.*

This is the motto of novum publishing, and our focus
is on finding new manuscripts, publishing them and
offering long-term support to the authors.
Our publishing house was founded in 1997, and since
then it has become THE expert for new authors and
has won numerous awards.

**Our editorial team will peruse each manuscript
within a few weeks free of charge and without
obligation.**

You will find more information about
novum publishing and our books on the internet:

w w w . n o v u m - p u b l i s h i n g . c o . u k

Solomon Aggrey

Following His Glory

ISBN 978-3-99107-732-9
236 pages

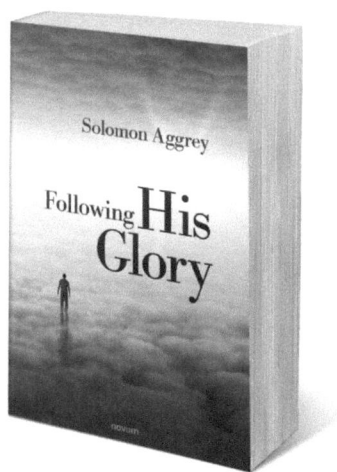

If the journey of the children of Israel from Egypt to the promise land is properly decoded, it will reveal the roadmap which is laid out for mankind; Following His Glory aims to provide the key to this biblical cipher.